# MznLnx

*Missing Links Exam Preps*

---

**Exam Prep for**

# International Management: Managing in a Diverse and Dynamic Global Environment

### Phatak et al..., 1st Edition

The MznLnx Exam Prep is your link from the texbook and lecture to your exams.
The MznLnx Exam Preps are unauthorized and comprehensive reviews of your textbooks.

All material provided by MznLnx and Rico Publications (c) 2010
Textbook publishers and textbook authors do not particpate in or contribute to these reviews.

# MznLnx

Rico
Publications

*Exam Prep for International Management: Managing in a Diverse and Dynamic Global Environment*
1st Edition
Phatak et al...

*Publisher:* Raymond Houge
*Assistant Editor:* Michael Rouger
*Text and Cover Designer:* Lisa Buckner
*Marketing Manager:* Sara Swagger
*Project Manager, Editorial Production:* Jerry Emerson
*Art Director:* Vernon Lowerui

*Product Manager:* Dave Mason
*Editorial Assitant:* Rachel Guzmanji
*Pedagogy:* Debra Long
*Cover Image:* Jim Reed/Getty Images
*Text and Cover Printer:* City Printing, Inc.
*Compositor:* Media Mix, Inc.

(c) 2010 Rico Publications
ALL RIGHTS RESERVED. No part of this work
covered by the copyright may be reproduced or
used in any form or by an means--graphic, electronic,
or mechanical, including photocopying, recording,
taping, Web distribution, information storage, and
retrieval systems, or in any other manner--without the
written permission of the publisher.

For more information about our products, contact us at:
Dave.Mason@RicoPublications.com

For permission to use material from this text or
product, submit a request online to:
Dave.Mason@RicoPublications.com

Printed in the United States
ISBN:

# Contents

**CHAPTER 1**
*An Introduction to International Management* — 1

**CHAPTER 2**
*The Global Macroeconomic Environment* — 10

**CHAPTER 3**
*The Political Environment and Political Risk* — 17

**CHAPTER 4**
*The International Legal Environment of Business* — 23

**CHAPTER 5**
*The Cultural Environment* — 28

**CHAPTER 6**
*Strategies for International Competition* — 32

**CHAPTER 7**
*Modes of Entry into Foreign Markets* — 40

**CHAPTER 8**
*Managing International Collaborative Initiatives* — 46

**CHAPTER 9**
*Organizing International Operations* — 49

**CHAPTER 10**
*Controlling International Strategies and Operations* — 50

**CHAPTER 11**
*Managing Technology and Knowledge* — 53

**CHAPTER 12**
*Communicating across Borders and Cultures* — 57

**CHAPTER 13**
*Negotiation and Decision Making across Borders and Cultures* — 58

**CHAPTER 14**
*Work Motivation across Cultures and Borders* — 60

**CHAPTER 15**
*Leadership across Borders and Cultures* — 65

**CHAPTER 16**
*International Human Resources Management* — 68

**CHAPTER 17**
*Ethics and Social Responsibility for International Firms* — 74

**ANSWER KEY** — 79

# TO THE STUDENT

### COMPREHENSIVE

The *MznLnx* Exam Prep series is designed to help you pass your exams. Editors at MznLnx review your textbooks and then prepare these practice exams to help you master the textbook material. Unlike study guides, workbooks, and practice tests provided by the texbook publisher and textbook authors, *MznLnx* gives you **all** of the material in each chapter in exam form, not just samples, so you can be sure to nail your exam.

### MECHANICAL

The MznLnx Exam Prep series creates exams that will help you learn the subject matter as well as test you on your understanding. Each question is designed to help you master the concept. Just working through the exams, you gain an understanding of the subject--its a simple mechanical process that produces success.

### INTEGRATED STUDY GUIDE AND REVIEW

MznLnx is not just a set of exams designed to test you, its also a comprehensive review of the subject content. Each exam question is also a review of the concept, making sure that you will get the answer correct without having to go to other sources of material. You learn as you go! Its the easiest way to pass an exam.

### HUMOR

Studying can be tedious and dry. MznLnx's instructional design includes moderate humor within the exam questions on occassion, to break the tedium and revitalize the brain

## Chapter 1. An Introduction to International Management

1. A _____ is one of several ways of doing research whether it is social science related or even socially related. It is an intensive study of a single group, incident, or community. Other ways include experiments, surveys, multiple histories, and analysis of archival information.

   Rather than using samples and following a rigid protocol to examine limited number of variables, _____ methods involve an in-depth, longitudinal examination of a single instance or event: a case.

   a. 1990 Clean Air Act
   b. Standard operating procedure
   c. Case study
   d. Longitudinal study

2. _____ is one of the managerial functions like planning, organizing, staffing and directing. It is an important function because it helps to check the errors and to take the corrective action so that deviation from standards are minimized and stated goals of the organization are achieved in desired manner. According to modern concepts, _____ is a foreseeing action whereas earlier concept of _____ was used only when errors were detected. _____ in management means setting standards, measuring actual performance and taking corrective action.

   a. Decision tree pruning
   b. Turnover
   c. Schedule of reinforcement
   d. Control

3. _____ is both the conscious and unconscious act of revealing more about ourselves to others. This may include but is not limited to thoughts, feelings, aspirations, goals, failures, successes, fears, dreams as well as our likes, dislikes, and favorites. Many people attempt to avoid 'self-disclosing' too much to coworkers, or when dating for fear of being judged negatively by others.

   a. Social network analysis
   b. Soft skill
   c. Self-disclosure
   d. Social influence

4. _____ in its classic form is defined as a company from one country making a physical investment into building a factory in another country. It is the establishment of an enterprise by a foreigner. Its definition can be extended to include investments made to acquire lasting interest in enterprises operating outside of the economy of the investor.

   a. Business Roundtable
   b. Headquarters
   c. Compensation methods
   d. Foreign direct investment

5. _____ is a form of corporate self-regulation integrated into a business model. Ideally, _____ policy would function as a built-in, self-regulating mechanism whereby business would monitor and ensure their adherence to law, ethical standards, and international norms. Business would embrace responsibility for the impact of their activities on the environment, consumers, employees, communities, stakeholders and all other members of the public sphere.
   a. 1990 Clean Air Act
   b. 33 Strategies of War
   c. Corporate social responsibility
   d. 28-hour day

6. The _____ or gross domestic income (GDI), a basic measure of an economy's economic performance, is the market value of all final goods and services made within the borders of a nation in a year. _____ can be defined in three ways, all of which are conceptually identical. First, it is equal to the total expenditures for all final goods and services produced within the country in a stipulated period of time (usually a 365-day year).
   a. Productivity management
   b. Perfect competition
   c. Human capital
   d. Gross domestic product

7. _____ is the amount of goods and services that a labourer produces in a given amount of time. It is one of several types of productivity that economists measure. _____ can be measured for a firm, a process or a country.
   a. Time and attendance
   b. Business Network Transformation
   c. Retroactive overtime
   d. Labour productivity

8. _____ refers to metrics and measures of output from production processes, per unit of input. Labor _____, for example, is typically measured as a ratio of output per labor-hour, an input. _____ may be conceived of as a metrics of the technical or engineering efficiency of production.
   a. Value engineering
   b. Master production schedule
   c. Productivity
   d. Remanufacturing

9. In decision theory and estimation theory, the _____ of an estimator, $\hat{\theta}$, of an unknown parameter of the distribution, θ, is the expected value of the loss function

## Chapter 1. An Introduction to International Management

$$R(\theta, \hat{\theta}) = \mathbb{E}_\theta L(\theta, \hat{\theta}) = \int L(\theta, \hat{\theta})\, dP_\theta.$$

where $dP_\theta$ is a probability measure parametrized by $\theta$.

- For a scalar parameter $\theta$ and a quadratic loss function,

$$L(\theta, \hat{\theta}) = (\theta - \hat{\theta})^2$$

the _____ function becomes the mean squared error of the estimate,

$$R(\theta, \hat{\theta}) = E_\theta (\theta - \hat{\theta})^2$$

- In density estimation, the unknown parameter is probability density itself. The loss function is typically chosen to be a norm in an appropriate function space. For example, for $L^2$ norm,

$$L(f, \hat{f}) = \|f - \hat{f}\|_2^2$$

the _____ function becomes the mean integrated squared error

$$R(f, \hat{f}) = E\|f - \hat{f}\|^2$$

a. Risk
b. Financial modeling
c. Linear model
d. Risk aversion

10. A _____ strategy is the planned method of delivering goods or services to a target market and distributing them there. When importing or exporting services, it refers to establishing and managing contracts in a foreign country.

Many companies successfully operate in a niche market without ever expanding into new markets.

a. Market entry
b. Psychological pricing
c. Foreign ownership
d. Horizontal integration

11. _____ is an advertisement in which a particular product specifically mentions a competitor by name for the express purpose of showing why the competitor is inferior to the product naming it.

This should not be confused with parody advertisements, where a fictional product is being advertised for the purpose of poking fun at the particular advertisement, nor should it be confused with the use of a coined brand name for the purpose of comparing the product without actually naming an actual competitor. ('Wikipedia tastes better and is less filling than the Encyclopedia Galactica.')

In the 1980s, during what has been referred to as the cola wars, soft-drink manufacturer Pepsi ran a series of advertisements where people, caught on hidden camera, in a blind taste test, chose Pepsi over rival Coca-Cola.

   a. 28-hour day
   b. Comparative advertising
   c. 33 Strategies of War
   d. 1990 Clean Air Act


12. A _____ is a process in which a potential employee is evaluated by an employer for prospective employment in their company, organization and was established in the late 16th century.

A _____ typically precedes the hiring decision, and is used to evaluate the candidate. The interview is usually preceded by the evaluation of submitted résumés from interested candidates, then selecting a small number of candidates for interviews.

   a. Split shift
   b. Job interview
   c. Payrolling
   d. Supported employment


13. _____ Management is the succession of strategies used by management as a product goes through its _____. The conditions in which a product is sold changes over time and must be managed as it moves through its succession of stages.

The _____ goes through many phases, involves many professional disciplines, and requires many skills, tools and processes.

   a. Job hunting
   b. Golden handshake
   c. Strategic Alliance
   d. Product life cycle

## Chapter 1. An Introduction to International Management

14. A _____ is a general term that describes any government policy or regulation that restricts international trade. The barriers can take many forms, including the following terms that include many restrictions in international trade within multiple countries that import and export any items of trade.

- Import duty
- Import licenses
- Export licenses
- Import quotas
- Tariffs
- Subsidies
- Non-tariff barriers to trade
- Voluntary Export Restraints
- Local Content Requirements
- Embargo

Most _____s work on the same principle: the imposition of some sort of cost on trade that raises the price of the traded products. If two or more nations repeatedly use _____s against each other, then a trade war results.

a. Trade creation
b. Customs brokerage
c. Most favoured nation
d. Trade barrier


15. The _____ is an international organization designed by its founders to supervise and liberalize international trade. The organization officially commenced on 1 January 1995, under the Marrakesh Agreement, succeeding the 1947 General Agreement on Tariffs and Trade (GATT.)

The _____ deals with regulation of trade between participating countries; it provides a framework for negotiating and formalising trade agreements, and a dispute resolution process aimed at enforcing participants' adherence to _____ agreements which are signed by representatives of member governments and ratified by their parliaments.

a. 1990 Clean Air Act
b. Network planning and design
c. National Institute for Occupational Safety and Health
d. World Trade Organization


16. In economics, business, retail, and accounting, a _____ is the value of money that has been used up to produce something, and hence is not available for use anymore. In economics, a _____ is an alternative that is given up as a result of a decision. In business, the _____ may be one of acquisition, in which case the amount of money expended to acquire it is counted as _____.

a. Fixed costs
b. Cost allocation
c. Cost overrun
d. Cost

17. _____ is the observation that people often do and believe things because many other people do and believe the same things. The effect is often called herd instinct. People tend to follow the crowd without examining the merits of a particular thing.
   a. Distinction bias
   b. Confirmation bias
   c. Choice-supportive bias
   d. Bandwagon effect

18. A _____ is a name or trademark connected with a product or producer. _____s have become increasingly important components of culture and the economy, now being described as 'cultural accessories and personal philosophies'.

Some people distinguish the psychological aspect of a _____ from the experiential aspect.

   a. Brand loyalty
   b. Brand awareness
   c. Brand extension
   d. Brand

19. Descriptive _____ assist in describing the distinguishable selling point(s) of the product to the customer (eg Snap Crackle ' Pop or Bitter Lemon.)

Associative _____ provide the customer with an associated word for what the product promises to do or be (e.g. Walkman, Sensodyne or Natrel)

Finally, Freestanding _____ have no links or ties to either descriptions or associations of use. (eg Mars Bar or Pantene)

The act of associating a product or service with a brand has become part of pop culture.

a. Brand extension
b. Brand awareness
c. Brand names
d. Brand image


20. In microeconomics and management, the term _____ describes a style of management control. Vertically integrated companies are united through a hierarchy with a common owner. Usually each member of the hierarchy produces a different product or (market-specific) service, and the products combine to satisfy a common need.
a. 28-hour day
b. 33 Strategies of War
c. 1990 Clean Air Act
d. Vertical integration


21. _____ is, in very basic words, a position a firm occupies against its competitors.

According to Michael Porter, the three methods for creating a sustainable _____ are through:

1. Cost leadership

2. Differentiation

3. Focus (economics)

a. 28-hour day
b. Competitive advantage
c. Theory Z
d. 1990 Clean Air Act


22. _____ as defined in business terms is an organization's strategic guide to globalization. A sound _____ should address these questions: what must be (versus what is) the extent of market presence in the world's major markets? How to build the necessary global presence? What must be (versus what is) the optimal locations around the world for the various value chain activities? How to run global presence into global competitive advantage?

Academic research on _____ came of age during the 1980s, including work by Michael Porter and Christopher Bartlett ' Sumantra Ghoshal. Among the forces perceived to bring about the globalization of competition were convergence in economic systems and technological change, especially in information technology, that facilitated and required the coordination of a multinational firm's strategy on a worldwide scale.

**Chapter 1. An Introduction to International Management**

a. 28-hour day
b. 33 Strategies of War
c. 1990 Clean Air Act
d. Global strategy

23. In economics, _____ refers to the ability of a person or a country to produce a particular good at a lower marginal cost and opportunity cost than another person or country. It is the ability to produce a product most efficiently given all the other products that could be produced. It can be contrasted with absolute advantage which refers to the ability of a person or a country to produce a particular good at a lower absolute cost than another.
   a. 28-hour day
   b. Comparative advantage
   c. 33 Strategies of War
   d. 1990 Clean Air Act

24. _____, in microeconomics, are the cost advantages that a business obtains due to expansion. They are factors that cause a producer's average cost per unit to fall as scale is increased. _____ is a long run concept and refers to reductions in unit cost as the size of a facility, or scale, increases.
   a. A4e
   b. A Stake in the Outcome
   c. Economies of scope
   d. Economies of scale

25. Network externalities resemble economies of scale, but they are not considered such because they are a function of the number of users of a good or service in an industry, not of the production efficiency within a business. _____ are only considered examples of network externalities if they are driven by demand side economies.

Formally, a production function is defined to have:

- constant returns to scale if (for any constant a greater than or equal to 0)
- increasing returns to scale if (for any constant a greater than 1)
- decreasing returns to scale if (for any constant a greater than 1)

where K and L are factors of production, capital and labour, respectively.

As an example, the Cobb-Douglas functional form has constant returns to scale when the sum of the exponents adds up to one.

a. AAAI
b. Economies of scale external to the firm
c. A Stake in the Outcome
d. A4e

## Chapter 2. The Global Macroeconomic Environment

1. A _____ is one of several ways of doing research whether it is social science related or even socially related. It is an intensive study of a single group, incident, or community. Other ways include experiments, surveys, multiple histories, and analysis of archival information.

Rather than using samples and following a rigid protocol to examine limited number of variables, _____ methods involve an in-depth, longitudinal examination of a single instance or event: a case.

   a. Longitudinal study
   b. 1990 Clean Air Act
   c. Standard operating procedure
   d. Case study


2. The _____ was the outcome of the failure of negotiating governments to create the International Trade Organization (ITO.) GATT was formed in 1947 and lasted until 1994, when it was replaced by the World Trade Organization. The Bretton Woods Conference had introduced the idea for an organization to regulate trade as part of a larger plan for economic recovery after World War II.

   a. 1990 Clean Air Act
   b. 28-hour day
   c. Multilateral treaty
   d. General Agreement on Tariffs and Trade


3. _____ in its literal sense is the process of transformation of local or regional phenomena into global ones. It can be described as a process by which the people of the world are unified into a single society and function together.

This process is a combination of economic, technological, sociocultural and political forces.

   a. Histogram
   b. Collaborative Planning, Forecasting and Replenishment
   c. Cost Management
   d. Globalization


4. The _____ is an international organization designed by its founders to supervise and liberalize international trade. The organization officially commenced on 1 January 1995, under the Marrakesh Agreement, succeeding the 1947 General Agreement on Tariffs and Trade (GATT.)

The _____ deals with regulation of trade between participating countries; it provides a framework for negotiating and formalising trade agreements, and a dispute resolution process aimed at enforcing participants' adherence to _____ agreements which are signed by representatives of member governments and ratified by their parliaments.

a. 1990 Clean Air Act
b. Network planning and design
c. World Trade Organization
d. National Institute for Occupational Safety and Health



5. A _____ is a customs union with common policies on product regulation, and freedom of movement of the factors of production (capital and labour) and of enterprise. The goal is that the movement of capital, labour, goods, and services between the members is as easy as within them. This is the fourth stage of economic integration.

a. Most favoured nation
b. Trade creation
c. Trade barrier
d. Common Market



6. _____ is a type of trade policy that allows traders to act and transact without interference from government. Thus, the policy permits trading partners mutual gains from trade, with goods and services produced according to the theory of comparative advantage.

Under a _____ policy, prices are a reflection of true supply and demand, and are the sole determinant of resource allocation.

a. 1990 Clean Air Act
b. 33 Strategies of War
c. 28-hour day
d. Free Trade



7. _____ is a designated group of countries that have agreed to eliminate tariffs, quotas and preferences on most (if not all) goods and services traded between them. It can be considered the second stage of economic integration. Countries choose this kind of economic integration form if their economical structures are complementary.

a. 28-hour day
b. 33 Strategies of War
c. Free trade area
d. 1990 Clean Air Act



8. The _____ is a trilateral trade bloc in North America created by the governments of the United States, Canada, and Mexico. The agreement creating the trade bloc came into force on January 1, 1994. It superseded the Canada-United States Free Trade Agreement between the U.S. and Canada.

a. North American Free Trade Agreement
b. Business war game
c. Career portfolios
d. Trade union

9. In decision theory and estimation theory, the _____ of an estimator, $\hat{\theta}$, of an unknown parameter of the distribution, θ, is the expected value of the loss function

$$R(\theta, \hat{\theta}) = \mathbb{E}_\theta L(\theta, \hat{\theta}) = \int L(\theta, \hat{\theta})\, dP_\theta.$$

where $dP_\theta$ is a probability measure parametrized by θ.

- For a scalar parameter θ and a quadratic loss function,

$$L(\theta, \hat{\theta}) = (\theta - \hat{\theta})^2$$

the _____ function becomes the mean squared error of the estimate,

$$R(\theta, \hat{\theta}) = E_\theta (\theta - \hat{\theta})^2$$

- In density estimation, the unknown parameter is probability density itself. The loss function is typically chosen to be a norm in an appropriate function space. For example, for $L^2$ norm,

$$L(f, \hat{f}) = \|f - \hat{f}\|_2^2$$

the _____ function becomes the mean integrated squared error

$$R(f, \hat{f}) = E\|f - \hat{f}\|^2$$

a. Risk aversion
b. Financial modeling
c. Linear model
d. Risk

## Chapter 2. The Global Macroeconomic Environment

10. _____ is an economic term related to international economics in which trade is created by the formation of a customs union.

When a customs union is formed, the member nations establish a free trade area amongst themselves and a common external tariff on non-member nations. As a result, the member nations establish greater trading ties between themselves now that protectionist barriers such as tariffs, quotas, and non-tariff barriers such as subsidies have been eliminated.

   a. Most favoured nation
   b. Trade creation
   c. Trade barrier
   d. Customs brokerage


11. _____, in microeconomics, are the cost advantages that a business obtains due to expansion. They are factors that cause a producer's average cost per unit to fall as scale is increased. _____ is a long run concept and refers to reductions in unit cost as the size of a facility, or scale, increases.

   a. A4e
   b. Economies of scope
   c. A Stake in the Outcome
   d. Economies of scale


12. A _____ is a process in which a potential employee is evaluated by an employer for prospective employment in their company, organization and was established in the late 16th century.

A _____ typically precedes the hiring decision, and is used to evaluate the candidate. The interview is usually preceded by the evaluation of submitted résumés from interested candidates, then selecting a small number of candidates for interviews.

   a. Job interview
   b. Supported employment
   c. Split shift
   d. Payrolling


13. _____ or worker mobility is the socioeconomic ease with which an individual or groups of individuals who are currently receiving remuneration in the form of wages can take advantage of various economic opportunities.

Worker mobility is best gauged by the lack of impediments to such mobility. Impediments to mobility are easily divided into two distinct classes with one being personal and the other being systemic.

**Chapter 2. The Global Macroeconomic Environment**

  a. 28-hour day
  b. Labor mobility
  c. 33 Strategies of War
  d. 1990 Clean Air Act

14. _____ refers to metrics and measures of output from production processes, per unit of input. Labor _____, for example, is typically measured as a ratio of output per labor-hour, an input. _____ may be conceived of as a metrics of the technical or engineering efficiency of production.
  a. Value engineering
  b. Remanufacturing
  c. Master production schedule
  d. Productivity

15. Network externalities resemble economies of scale, but they are not considered such because they are a function of the number of users of a good or service in an industry, not of the production efficiency within a business. _____ are only considered examples of network externalities if they are driven by demand side economies.

Formally, a production function $f$ is defined to have:

- constant returns to scale if (for any constant a greater than or equal to 0) $f(aK, aL) = af(K, L)$
- increasing returns to scale if (for any constant a greater than 1) $f(aK, aL) > af(K, L)$
- decreasing returns to scale if (for any constant a greater than 1) $f(aK, aL) < af(K, L)$

where K and L are factors of production, capital and labour, respectively.

As an example, the Cobb-Douglas functional form has constant returns to scale when the sum of the exponents adds up to one.

  a. A Stake in the Outcome
  b. Economies of scale external to the firm
  c. A4e
  d. AAAI

## Chapter 2. The Global Macroeconomic Environment

16. The _____ movement is critical of the globalization of capitalism. The movement is also commonly referred to as the global justice movement, alter-globalization movement, anti-corporate globalization movement, or movement against neoliberal globalization. Corresponding terms in other languages are mouvement altermondialiste , globalisierungskritische Bewegung , or Movimento no-global (Italian.)
   a. A4e
   b. A Stake in the Outcome
   c. AAAI
   d. Anti-globalization

17. _____ is exchange of capital, goods, and services across international borders or territories. In most countries, it represents a significant share of gross domestic product (GDP.) While _____ has been present throughout much of history , its economic, social, and political importance has been on the rise in recent centuries.
   a. A Stake in the Outcome
   b. International trade
   c. AAAI
   d. A4e

18. In economics, business, retail, and accounting, a _____ is the value of money that has been used up to produce something, and hence is not available for use anymore. In economics, a _____ is an alternative that is given up as a result of a decision. In business, the _____ may be one of acquisition, in which case the amount of money expended to acquire it is counted as _____.
   a. Cost allocation
   b. Fixed costs
   c. Cost overrun
   d. Cost

19. In economics, the people in the _____ are the suppliers of labor. The _____ is all the nonmilitary people who are employed or unemployed. In 2005, the worldwide _____ was over 3 billion people.
   a. Labor force
   b. Pink-collar worker
   c. Departmentalization
   d. Decent work

20. A _____ is typically described as a deliberate plan of action to guide decisions and achieve rational outcome(s.) However, the term may also be used to denote what is actually done, even though it is unplanned.

The term may apply to government, private sector organizations and groups, and individuals.

a. 1990 Clean Air Act
b. 28-hour day
c. Policy
d. 33 Strategies of War

21. A _____ or transnational corporation is a corporation or enterprise that manages production or delivers services in more than one country. It can also be referred to as an international corporation.

The first modern _____ is generally thought to be the Dutch East India Company, established in 1602.

a. Small and medium enterprises
b. Command center
c. Financial Accounting Standards Board
d. Multinational corporation

22. The _____ Automobile Company is an automobile manufacturer based in Wolfsburg, Germany, and is the original brand within the _____ Group, as well as the largest brand by sales volume.

_____ means 'people's car' in German, in which it is pronounced . Its current tagline or slogan is Das Auto .

a. Volkswagen
b. Rate of return
c. Competence-based Strategic Management
d. Turnover

23. _____ is a broad label that refers to any individuals or households that use goods and services generated within the economy. The concept of a _____ is used in different contexts, so that the usage and significance of the term may vary.

Typically when business people and economists talk of _____s they are talking about person as _____, an aggregated commodity item with little individuality other than that expressed in the buy/not-buy decision.

a. 28-hour day
b. 1990 Clean Air Act
c. 33 Strategies of War
d. Consumer

## Chapter 3. The Political Environment and Political Risk

1. In decision theory and estimation theory, the _____ of an estimator, $\hat{\theta}$, of an unknown parameter of the distribution, θ, is the expected value of the loss function

$$R(\theta, \hat{\theta}) = \mathbb{E}_\theta L(\theta, \hat{\theta}) = \int L(\theta, \hat{\theta})\, dP_\theta.$$

where $dP_\theta$ is a probability measure parametrized by θ.

- For a scalar parameter θ and a quadratic loss function,

$$L(\theta, \hat{\theta}) = (\theta - \hat{\theta})^2$$

the _____ function becomes the mean squared error of the estimate,

$$R(\theta, \hat{\theta}) = E_\theta (\theta - \hat{\theta})^2$$

- In density estimation, the unknown parameter is probability density itself. The loss function is typically chosen to be a norm in an appropriate function space. For example, for $L^2$ norm,

$$L(f, \hat{f}) = \|f - \hat{f}\|_2^2$$

the _____ function becomes the mean integrated squared error

$$R(f, \hat{f}) = E\|f - \hat{f}\|^2$$

a. Financial modeling
b. Risk aversion
c. Linear model
d. Risk

2. A _____ is someone who helps a group of people understand their common objectives and assists them to plan to achieve them without taking a particular position in the discussion. The _____ will try to assist the group in achieving a consensus on any disagreements that preexist or emerge in the meeting so that it has a strong basis for future action. The role has been likened to that of a midwife who assists in the process of birth but is not the producer of the end result.

a. 33 Strategies of War
b. Facilitator
c. 1990 Clean Air Act
d. 28-hour day



3. A _____ is typically described as a deliberate plan of action to guide decisions and achieve rational outcome(s.) However, the term may also be used to denote what is actually done, even though it is unplanned.

The term may apply to government, private sector organizations and groups, and individuals.

a. 1990 Clean Air Act
b. Policy
c. 33 Strategies of War
d. 28-hour day


4. _____ is both the conscious and unconscious act of revealing more about ourselves to others. This may include but is not limited to thoughts, feelings, aspirations, goals, failures, successes, fears, dreams as well as our likes, dislikes, and favorites. Many people attempt to avoid 'self-disclosing' too much to coworkers, or when dating for fear of being judged negatively by others.
a. Soft skill
b. Social network analysis
c. Social influence
d. Self-disclosure


5. _____ is the process of estimation in unknown situations. Prediction is a similar, but more general term. Both can refer to estimation of time series, cross-sectional or longitudinal data.
a. 1990 Clean Air Act
b. 33 Strategies of War
c. Forecasting
d. 28-hour day


6. The _____ is an international organization designed by its founders to supervise and liberalize international trade. The organization officially commenced on 1 January 1995, under the Marrakesh Agreement, succeeding the 1947 General Agreement on Tariffs and Trade (GATT.)

## Chapter 3. The Political Environment and Political Risk

The _____ deals with regulation of trade between participating countries; it provides a framework for negotiating and formalising trade agreements, and a dispute resolution process aimed at enforcing participants' adherence to _____ agreements which are signed by representatives of member governments and ratified by their parliaments.

a. World Trade Organization
b. 1990 Clean Air Act
c. Network planning and design
d. National Institute for Occupational Safety and Health

7. A command economy or directed economy is an economic system in which the government or workers' councils manages the economy. It is an economic system in which the central government makes all decisions on the production and consumption of goods and services. Its most extensive form is referred to as a command economy, _____, or command and control economy.

a. 28-hour day
b. Market economies
c. 1990 Clean Air Act
d. Centrally planned economy

8. An _____ is a risk arising from execution of a company's business functions. As such, it is a very broad concept including e.g. fraud risks, legal risks, physical or environmental risks, etc. The term _____ is most commonly found in risk management programs of financial institutions that must organize their risk management program according to Basel II.

a. A4e
b. Operational risk
c. AAAI
d. A Stake in the Outcome

9. _____ is the state or fact of exclusive rights and control over property, which may be an object, land/real estate or intellectual property. An _____ right is also referred to as title. The concept of _____ has existed for thousands of years and in all cultures.

a. A Stake in the Outcome
b. Emanation of the state
c. A4e
d. Ownership

10. _____ is a concept related to the relative abilities of parties in a situation to exert influence over each other. If both parties are on an equal footing in a debate, then they will have equal _____, such as in a perfectly competitive market, or between an evenly matched monopoly and monopsony.

There are a number of fields where the concept of _____ has proven crucial to coherent analysis: game theory, labour economics, collective bargaining arrangements, diplomatic negotiations, settlement of litigation, the price of insurance, and any negotiation in general.

   a. Bargaining power
   b. Buy-sell agreement
   c. Trade credit
   d. 1990 Clean Air Act

11. A _____ strategy is the planned method of delivering goods or services to a target market and distributing them there. When importing or exporting services, it refers to establishing and managing contracts in a foreign country.

Many companies successfully operate in a niche market without ever expanding into new markets.

   a. Market entry
   b. Psychological pricing
   c. Foreign ownership
   d. Horizontal integration

12. A _____ is an entity formed between two or more parties to undertake economic activity together. The parties agree to create a new entity by both contributing equity, and they then share in the revenues, expenses, and control of the enterprise. The venture can be for one specific project only, or a continuing business relationship such as the Fuji Xerox _____.
   a. Civil Rights Act of 1991
   b. Meritor Savings Bank v. Vinson
   c. Patent
   d. Joint venture

13. An _____ is a person who has possession of an enterprise and assumes significant accountability for the inherent risks and the outcome. It is an ambitious leader who combines land, labor, and capital to create and market new goods or services. The term is a loanword from French and was first defined by the Irish economist Richard Cantillon.

a. A4e
b. Entrepreneur
c. A Stake in the Outcome
d. AAAI

14. In economics, business, retail, and accounting, a _____ is the value of money that has been used up to produce something, and hence is not available for use anymore. In economics, a _____ is an alternative that is given up as a result of a decision. In business, the _____ may be one of acquisition, in which case the amount of money expended to acquire it is counted as _____.
a. Cost overrun
b. Fixed costs
c. Cost allocation
d. Cost

15. A _____ is a relatively new executive level position at a corporation, company, organization typically reporting directly to the CEO or board of directors. The _____ is responsible for a brand's image, experience, and promise, and propagating it throughout all aspects of the company. The brand officer oversees marketing, advertising, design, public relations and customer service departments.
a. Chief executive officer
b. Director of communications
c. Purchasing manager
d. Chief brand officer

16. The act of becoming a surety is also called a _____. Traditionally a _____ was distinguished from a surety in that the surety's liability was joint and primary with the principal, whereas the guaranty's liability was ancillary and derivative, but many jurisdictions have abolished this distinction
a. Blue sky law
b. Clayton Antitrust Act
c. National treatment
d. Guarantee

17. A _____ is one of several ways of doing research whether it is social science related or even socially related. It is an intensive study of a single group, incident, or community. Other ways include experiments, surveys, multiple histories, and analysis of archival information .

Rather than using samples and following a rigid protocol to examine limited number of variables, _____ methods involve an in-depth, longitudinal examination of a single instance or event: a case.

a. Case study
b. 1990 Clean Air Act
c. Standard operating procedure
d. Longitudinal study

## Chapter 4. The International Legal Environment of Business

1. A _____ is one of several ways of doing research whether it is social science related or even socially related. It is an intensive study of a single group, incident, or community. Other ways include experiments, surveys, multiple histories, and analysis of archival information.

Rather than using samples and following a rigid protocol to examine limited number of variables, _____ methods involve an in-depth, longitudinal examination of a single instance or event: a case.

   a. 1990 Clean Air Act
   b. Longitudinal study
   c. Standard operating procedure
   d. Case study

2. A _____ is a list of the general tasks and responsibilities of a position. Typically, it also includes to whom the position reports, specifications such as the qualifications needed by the person in the job, salary range for the position, etc. A _____ is usually developed by conducting a job analysis, which includes examining the tasks and sequences of tasks necessary to perform the job.
   a. Recruitment
   b. Recruitment Process Insourcing
   c. Recruitment advertising
   d. Job description

3. _____ are legal property rights over creations of the mind, both artistic and commercial, and the corresponding fields of law. Under _____ law, owners are granted certain exclusive rights to a variety of intangible assets, such as musical, literary, and artistic works; ideas, discoveries and inventions; and words, phrases, symbols, and designs. Common types of _____ include copyrights, trademarks, patents, industrial design rights and trade secrets.
   a. Unemployment Action Center
   b. Equal Pay Act
   c. Intent
   d. Intellectual property

4. _____ plant, and equipment, is a term used in accountancy for assets and property which cannot easily be converted into cash. This can be compared with current assets such as cash or bank accounts, which are described as liquid assets. In most cases, only tangible assets are referred to as fixed.
   a. 28-hour day
   b. Fixed asset
   c. 1990 Clean Air Act
   d. 33 Strategies of War

## Chapter 4. The International Legal Environment of Business

5. The _____ is an international organization designed by its founders to supervise and liberalize international trade. The organization officially commenced on 1 January 1995, under the Marrakesh Agreement, succeeding the 1947 General Agreement on Tariffs and Trade (GATT.)

The _____ deals with regulation of trade between participating countries; it provides a framework for negotiating and formalising trade agreements, and a dispute resolution process aimed at enforcing participants' adherence to _____ agreements which are signed by representatives of member governments and ratified by their parliaments.

   a. World Trade Organization
   b. 1990 Clean Air Act
   c. Network planning and design
   d. National Institute for Occupational Safety and Health


6. A _____ is a formal relationship between two or more parties to pursue a set of agreed upon goals or to meet a critical business need while remaining independent organizations.

Partners may provide the _____ with resources such as products, distribution channels, manufacturing capability, project funding, capital equipment, knowledge, expertise, or intellectual property. The alliance is a cooperation or collaboration which aims for a synergy where each partner hopes that the benefits from the alliance will be greater than those from individual efforts.

   a. Golden parachute
   b. Process automation
   c. Farmshoring
   d. Strategic alliance


7. The _____, also conveniently known as the Madrid system or simply Madrid, is the primary international system for facilitating the registration of trademarks in multiple jurisdictions around the world.

The Madrid system provides a centrally administered system of obtaining a bundle of trademark registrations in separate jurisdictions. Registration through the Madrid system does not create an 'international' registration, as in the case of the European CTM system, rather it creates a bundle of national rights, able to be administered centrally.

   a. Federal Trade Commission Act
   b. Copyright Act of 1976
   c. Family and Medical Leave Act of 1993
   d. Madrid system for the international registration of marks

## Chapter 4. The International Legal Environment of Business

8. _____ is a status awarded by one nation to another in international trade. It means that the receiving nation will be granted all trade advantages -- such as low tariffs -- that any other nation also receives. In effect, a nation with _____ status will not be treated worse than any other nation with _____ status.

   a. Trade barrier
   b. Customs brokerage
   c. Trade creation
   d. Most favoured nation

9. _____ is a principle in customary international law vital to many treaty regimes. It essentially means treating foreigners and locals equally. Under _____, if a state grants a particular right, benefit or privilege to its own citizens, it must also grant those advantages to the citizens of other states while they are in that country.

   a. Pareto Principle
   b. Product liability
   c. National treatment
   d. Leave of absence

10. A _____ is one scenario provided for evaluation by respondents in a Choice Experiment. Responses are collected and used to create a Choice Model. Respondents are usually provided with a series of differing _____s for evaluation.

    a. Pairwise comparison
    b. Computerized classification test
    c. Thurstone scale
    d. Choice Set

11. A _____ is a set of exclusive rights granted by a state to an inventor or his assignee for a limited period of time in exchange for a disclosure of an invention.

    The procedure for granting _____s, the requirements placed on the _____ee and the extent of the exclusive rights vary widely between countries according to national laws and international agreements. Typically, however, a _____ application must include one or more claims defining the invention which must be new, inventive, and useful or industrially applicable.

    a. Labor Management Reporting and Disclosure Act
    b. Patent
    c. Food, Drug, and Cosmetic Act
    d. Federal Trade Commission Act

## Chapter 4. The International Legal Environment of Business

12. The _____, signed in Paris, France, on March 20, 1883, was one of the first intellectual property treaties. As a result of this treaty, intellectual property systems, including patents, of any contracting state are accessible to the nationals of other states party to the Convention.

The 'Convention priority right', also called 'Paris Convention priority right' or 'Union priority right', was also established by this treaty.

   a. 33 Strategies of War
   b. Paris Convention for the Protection of Industrial Property
   c. 28-hour day
   d. 1990 Clean Air Act

13. A _____ is a distinctive sign or indicator used by an individual, business organization, or other legal entity to identify that the products and/or services to consumers with which the _____ appears originate from a unique source and to distinguish its products or services from those of other entities.
   a. Succession planning
   b. Kanban
   c. Virtual team
   d. Trademark

14. _____ is a type of trade policy that allows traders to act and transact without interference from government. Thus, the policy permits trading partners mutual gains from trade, with goods and services produced according to the theory of comparative advantage.

Under a _____ policy, prices are a reflection of true supply and demand, and are the sole determinant of resource allocation.

   a. 1990 Clean Air Act
   b. Free trade
   c. 28-hour day
   d. 33 Strategies of War

15. The _____ of 1977 (15 U.S.C. §§ 78dd-1, et seq.) is a United States federal law known primarily for two of its main provisions, one that addresses accounting transparency requirements under the Securities Exchange Act of 1934 and another concerning bribery of foreign officials.

a. Limited liability
b. Foreign Corrupt Practices Act
c. Social Security Act of 1965
d. Meritor Savings Bank v. Vinson

## Chapter 5. The Cultural Environment

1. A _____ is one of several ways of doing research whether it is social science related or even socially related. It is an intensive study of a single group, incident, or community. Other ways include experiments, surveys, multiple histories, and analysis of archival information.

   Rather than using samples and following a rigid protocol to examine limited number of variables, _____ methods involve an in-depth, longitudinal examination of a single instance or event: a case.

   a. Standard operating procedure
   b. Longitudinal study
   c. 1990 Clean Air Act
   d. Case study


2. A _____ is a list of the general tasks and responsibilities of a position. Typically, it also includes to whom the position reports, specifications such as the qualifications needed by the person in the job, salary range for the position, etc. A _____ is usually developed by conducting a job analysis, which includes examining the tasks and sequences of tasks necessary to perform the job.
   a. Job description
   b. Recruitment
   c. Recruitment advertising
   d. Recruitment Process Insourcing


3. The _____ captures an expanded spectrum of values and criteria for measuring organizational success: economic, ecological and social. With the ratification of the United Nations and ICLEI _____ standard for urban and community accounting in early 2007, this became the dominant approach to public sector full cost accounting. Similar UN standards apply to natural capital and human capital measurement to assist in measurements required by _____, e.g. the ecoBudget standard for reporting ecological footprint.
   a. 1990 Clean Air Act
   b. Triple bottom line
   c. 33 Strategies of War
   d. 28-hour day


4. _____ is a term used to describe any moral, political that stresses human interdependence and the importance of a collective, rather than the importance of separate individuals. Collectivists focus on community and society, and seek to give priority to group goals over individual goals. The philosophical underpinnings of _____ are for some related to holism or organicism - the view that the whole is greater than the sum of its parts/pieces.
   a. 28-hour day
   b. Collaborative methods
   c. Collectivism
   d. 1990 Clean Air Act

## Chapter 5. The Cultural Environment

5. _____-model (SCOR(r)) is a process reference model developed by the management consulting firm PRTM and AMR Research and endorsed by the Supply-Chain Council (SCC) as the cross-industry de facto standard diagnostic tool for supply chain management. SCOR enables users to address, improve, and communicate supply chain management practices within and between all interested parties in the Extended Enterprise.

SCOR(r) is a management tool, spanning from the supplier's supplier to the customer's customer. The model has been developed by the members of the Council on a volunteer basis to describe the business activities associated with all phases of satisfying a customer's demand.

   a. Supply-Chain Operations Reference
   b. Supply Chain Risk Management
   c. Supply chain management software
   d. Delayed differentiation


6. Various _____ can be employed dependent on the culture of the business, the nature of the task, the nature of the workforce and the personality and skills of the leaders. This idea was further developed by Robert Tannenbaum and Warren H. Schmidt (1958, 1973) who argued that the style of leadership is dependent upon the prevailing circumstance; therefore leaders should exercise a range of leadership styles and should deploy them as appropriate.

An Autocratic or authoritarian manager makes all the decisions, keeping the information and decision making among the senior management.

   a. 33 Strategies of War
   b. Management styles
   c. 1990 Clean Air Act
   d. 28-hour day


7. _____ is a range of processes aimed at alleviating or eliminating sources of conflict. The term '_____' is sometimes used interchangeably with the term dispute resolution or alternative dispute resolution. Processes of _____ generally include negotiation, mediation and diplomacy.
   a. Conflict resolution
   b. 33 Strategies of War
   c. 28-hour day
   d. 1990 Clean Air Act


8. _____ is a type of trade policy that allows traders to act and transact without interference from government. Thus, the policy permits trading partners mutual gains from trade, with goods and services produced according to the theory of comparative advantage.

Under a _____ policy, prices are a reflection of true supply and demand, and are the sole determinant of resource allocation.

a. Free Trade
b. 33 Strategies of War
c. 1990 Clean Air Act
d. 28-hour day

9. _____ is a designated group of countries that have agreed to eliminate tariffs, quotas and preferences on most (if not all) goods and services traded between them. It can be considered the second stage of economic integration. Countries choose this kind of economic integration form if their economical structures are complementary.
a. 1990 Clean Air Act
b. 33 Strategies of War
c. Free trade area
d. 28-hour day

10. The _____ is a trilateral trade bloc in North America created by the governments of the United States, Canada, and Mexico. The agreement creating the trade bloc came into force on January 1, 1994. It superseded the Canada-United States Free Trade Agreement between the U.S. and Canada.
a. North American Free Trade Agreement
b. Career portfolios
c. Trade union
d. Business war game

11. _____ is an advertisement in which a particular product specifically mentions a competitor by name for the express purpose of showing why the competitor is inferior to the product naming it.

This should not be confused with parody advertisements, where a fictional product is being advertised for the purpose of poking fun at the particular advertisement, nor should it be confused with the use of a coined brand name for the purpose of comparing the product without actually naming an actual competitor. ('Wikipedia tastes better and is less filling than the Encyclopedia Galactica.')

In the 1980s, during what has been referred to as the cola wars, soft-drink manufacturer Pepsi ran a series of advertisements where people, caught on hidden camera, in a blind taste test, chose Pepsi over rival Coca-Cola.

a. 33 Strategies of War
b. Comparative advertising
c. 1990 Clean Air Act
d. 28-hour day

## Chapter 6. Strategies for International Competition

1. A _____ is one of several ways of doing research whether it is social science related or even socially related. It is an intensive study of a single group, incident, or community. Other ways include experiments, surveys, multiple histories, and analysis of archival information.

Rather than using samples and following a rigid protocol to examine limited number of variables, _____ methods involve an in-depth, longitudinal examination of a single instance or event: a case.

   a. Longitudinal study
   b. Standard operating procedure
   c. 1990 Clean Air Act
   d. Case study


2. _____ is the principle of organization of a region around several political, social or financial centres. An example of a polycentric city is the Ruhr area in Germany: Today, the area is a large city that grew from a dozen smaller cities. As a result, the 'city' has no single centre, but several.
   a. Polycentrism
   b. 1990 Clean Air Act
   c. 33 Strategies of War
   d. 28-hour day


3. The _____ is a concept from business management that was first described and popularized by Michael Porter in his 1985 best-seller, Competitive Advantage: Creating and Sustaining Superior Performance.

A _____ is a chain of activities. Products pass through all activities of the chain in order and at each activity the product gains some value. The chain of activities gives the products more added value than the sum of added values of all activities. It is important not to mix the concept of the _____ with the costs occurring throughout the activities.

   a. Customer relationship management
   b. Market development
   c. Mass marketing
   d. Value chain


4. A _____ is someone who helps a group of people understand their common objectives and assists them to plan to achieve them without taking a particular position in the discussion. The _____ will try to assist the group in achieving a consensus on any disagreements that preexist or emerge in the meeting so that it has a strong basis for future action. The role has been likened to that of a midwife who assists in the process of birth but is not the producer of the end result.

## Chapter 6. Strategies for International Competition

a. 28-hour day
b. 33 Strategies of War
c. 1990 Clean Air Act
d. Facilitator

5. The _____ is the weighted-average most likely outcome in gambling, probability theory, economics or finance.

What Does _____ Mean? The average of a probability distribution of possible returns, calculated by using the following formula:

E(R)= Sum: probability (in scenario i) * the return (in scenario i)

How do you calculate the average of a probability distribution? As denoted by the above formula, simply take the probability of each possible return outcome and multiply it by the return outcome itself. For example, if you knew a given investment had a 50% chance of earning a 10% return, a 25% chance of earning 20% and a 25% chance of earning -10%, the _____ would be equal to 7.5%:

= (0.5) (0.1) + (0.25) (0.2) + (0.25) (-0.1) = 0.075 = 7.5%

Although this is what you expect the return to be, there is no guarantee that it will be the actual return.

a. Expected gain
b. Inflation rate
c. Open compensation plan
d. Expected return

6. In decision theory and estimation theory, the _____ of an estimator, $\hat{\theta}$, of an unknown parameter of the distribution, θ, is the expected value of the loss function

$$R(\theta, \hat{\theta}) = \mathbb{E}_\theta L(\theta, \hat{\theta}) = \int L(\theta, \hat{\theta})\, dP_\theta.$$

where dP$_\theta$ is a probability measure parametrized by θ.

- For a scalar parameter θ and a quadratic loss function,

$$L(\theta, \hat{\theta}) = (\theta - \hat{\theta})^2$$

the _____ function becomes the mean squared error of the estimate,

$$R(\theta, \hat{\theta}) = E_\theta (\theta - \hat{\theta})^2$$

- In density estimation, the unknown parameter is probability density itself. The loss function is typically chosen to be a norm in an appropriate function space. For example, for L$^2$ norm,

$$L(f, \hat{f}) = \|f - \hat{f}\|_2^2$$

the _____ function becomes the mean integrated squared error

$$R(f, \hat{f}) = E\|f - \hat{f}\|^2$$

a. Linear model
b. Financial modeling
c. Risk
d. Risk aversion


7. A _____ strategy is the planned method of delivering goods or services to a target market and distributing them there. When importing or exporting services, it refers to establishing and managing contracts in a foreign country.

Many companies successfully operate in a niche market without ever expanding into new markets.

a. Market entry
b. Psychological pricing
c. Horizontal integration
d. Foreign ownership

## Chapter 6. Strategies for International Competition

8. A _____ is an entity formed between two or more parties to undertake economic activity together. The parties agree to create a new entity by both contributing equity, and they then share in the revenues, expenses, and control of the enterprise. The venture can be for one specific project only, or a continuing business relationship such as the Fuji Xerox _____.

   a. Meritor Savings Bank v. Vinson
   b. Joint venture
   c. Patent
   d. Civil Rights Act of 1991

9. A _____ is a formal relationship between two or more parties to pursue a set of agreed upon goals or to meet a critical business need while remaining independent organizations.

   Partners may provide the _____ with resources such as products, distribution channels, manufacturing capability, project funding, capital equipment, knowledge, expertise, or intellectual property. The alliance is a cooperation or collaboration which aims for a synergy where each partner hopes that the benefits from the alliance will be greater than those from individual efforts.

   a. Farmshoring
   b. Process automation
   c. Golden parachute
   d. Strategic alliance

10. An _____ is a person who has possession of an enterprise and assumes significant accountability for the inherent risks and the outcome. It is an ambitious leader who combines land, labor, and capital to create and market new goods or services. The term is a loanword from French and was first defined by the Irish economist Richard Cantillon.

    a. AAAI
    b. A Stake in the Outcome
    c. A4e
    d. Entrepreneur

11. Procter is a surname, and may also refer to:

    - Bryan Waller Procter (pseud. Barry Cornwall), English poet
    - Goodwin Procter, American law firm
    - _____, consumer products multinational

## Chapter 6. Strategies for International Competition

a. Procter ' Gamble
b. Strict liability
c. Downstream
d. Master and Servant Acts

12. _____ is one of the managerial functions like planning, organizing, staffing and directing. It is an important function because it helps to check the errors and to take the corrective action so that deviation from standards are minimized and stated goals of the organization are achieved in desired manner. According to modern concepts, _____ is a foreseeing action whereas earlier concept of _____ was used only when errors were detected. _____ in management means setting standards, measuring actual performance and taking corrective action.

a. Decision tree pruning
b. Schedule of reinforcement
c. Turnover
d. Control

13. _____ can be regarded as an outcome of mental processes (cognitive process) leading to the selection of a course of action among several alternatives. Every _____ process produces a final choice. The output can be an action or an opinion of choice.

a. Decision making
b. 28-hour day
c. 33 Strategies of War
d. 1990 Clean Air Act

14. A _____ is a process in which a potential employee is evaluated by an employer for prospective employment in their company, organization and was established in the late 16th century.

A _____ typically precedes the hiring decision, and is used to evaluate the candidate. The interview is usually preceded by the evaluation of submitted résumés from interested candidates, then selecting a small number of candidates for interviews.

a. Supported employment
b. Split shift
c. Payrolling
d. Job interview

15. _____ is, in very basic words, a position a firm occupies against its competitors.

According to Michael Porter, the three methods for creating a sustainable _____ are through:

## Chapter 6. Strategies for International Competition

1. Cost leadership

2. Differentiation

3. Focus (economics)

   a. 28-hour day
   b. Competitive advantage
   c. 1990 Clean Air Act
   d. Theory Z


16. _____ in manufacturing refers to processes that occur later on in a production sequence or production line.

Viewing a company 'from order to cash' might have high-level processes such as Marketing, Sales, Order Entry, Manufacturing, Packaging, Shipping, Invoicing. Each of these could be deconstructed into many sub-processes and supporting processes.

   a. Science Learning Centre
   b. Genbutsu
   c. Probability-generating function
   d. Downstream


17. _____ is a dynamic of being mutually and physically responsible to and sharing a common set of principles with others. This concept differs distinctly from 'dependence' in that an interdependent relationship implies that all participants are emotionally, economically, ecologically and or morally 'interdependent.' Some people advocate freedom or independence as a sort of ultimate good; others do the same with devotion to one's family, community, or society. _____ recognizes the truth in each position and weaves them together.
   a. AAAI
   b. A Stake in the Outcome
   c. Interdependence
   d. A4e


18. _____ is subcontracting a process, such as product design or manufacturing, to a third-party company. The decision to outsource is often made in the interest of lowering cost or making better use of time and energy costs, redirecting or conserving energy directed at the competencies of a particular business, or to make more efficient use of land, labor, capital, (information) technology and resources. _____ became part of the business lexicon during the 1980s.

## Chapter 6. Strategies for International Competition

a. Operant conditioning
b. Unemployment insurance
c. Opinion leadership
d. Outsourcing

19. _____ is something that a firm can do well and that meets the following three conditions:

Competencies are things that companys execute well across several business units or product sectors.

Firms usually have few competencies, but these are usually less liable to change rapidly.

1. It provides consumer benefits
2. It is not easy for competitors to imitate
3. It can be leveraged widely to many products and markets.

A _____ can take various forms, including technical/subject matter know-how, a reliable process and/or close relationships with customers and suppliers (Mascarenhas et al. 1998.)

a. NAIRU
b. Learning-by-doing
c. Core competency
d. Dominant Design

20. _____ refers to the movement of cash into or out of a business or financial product. It is usually measured during a specified, finite period of time. Measurement of _____ can be used

- to determine a project's rate of return or value. The time of _____s into and out of projects are used as inputs in financial models such as internal rate of return, and net present value.
- to determine problems with a business's liquidity. Being profitable does not necessarily mean being liquid. A company can fail because of a shortage of cash, even while profitable.
- as an alternate measure of a business's profits when it is believed that accrual accounting concepts do not represent economic realities. For example, a company may be notionally profitable but generating little operational cash (as may be the case for a company that barters its products rather than selling for cash.) In such a case, the company may be deriving additional operating cash by issuing shares evaluating default risk, re-investment requirements, etc.

_____ is a generic term used differently depending on the context. It may be defined by users for their own purposes.

a. Gross profit margin
b. Gross profit
c. Sweat equity
d. Cash flow

21. The _____ of an edge is $c_f(u, v) = c(u, v) - f(u, v)$. This defines a residual network denoted $G_f(V, E_f)$, giving the amount of available capacity. See that there can be an edge from $u$ to $v$ in the residual network, even though there is no edge from $u$ to $v$ in the original network.

a. 28-hour day
b. 33 Strategies of War
c. 1990 Clean Air Act
d. Residual capacity

22. _____ as defined in business terms is an organization's strategic guide to globalization. A sound _____ should address these questions: what must be (versus what is) the extent of market presence in the world's major markets? How to build the necessary global presence? What must be (versus what is) the optimal locations around the world for the various value chain activities? How to run global presence into global competitive advantage?

Academic research on _____ came of age during the 1980s, including work by Michael Porter and Christopher Bartlett ' Sumantra Ghoshal. Among the forces perceived to bring about the globalization of competition were convergence in economic systems and technological change, especially in information technology, that facilitated and required the coordination of a multinational firm's strategy on a worldwide scale.

a. 1990 Clean Air Act
b. 33 Strategies of War
c. 28-hour day
d. Global strategy

23. _____ in its literal sense is the process of transformation of local or regional phenomena into global ones. It can be described as a process by which the people of the world are unified into a single society and function together.

This process is a combination of economic, technological, sociocultural and political forces.

a. Histogram
b. Cost Management
c. Collaborative Planning, Forecasting and Replenishment
d. Globalization

## Chapter 7. Modes of Entry into Foreign Markets

1. A _____ is one of several ways of doing research whether it is social science related or even socially related. It is an intensive study of a single group, incident, or community. Other ways include experiments, surveys, multiple histories, and analysis of archival information .

Rather than using samples and following a rigid protocol to examine limited number of variables, _____ methods involve an in-depth, longitudinal examination of a single instance or event: a case.

   a. Longitudinal study
   b. Standard operating procedure
   c. 1990 Clean Air Act
   d. Case study


2. _____ is exchange of capital, goods, and services across international borders or territories. In most countries, it represents a significant share of gross domestic product (GDP.) While _____ has been present throughout much of history , its economic, social, and political importance has been on the rise in recent centuries.
   a. A Stake in the Outcome
   b. International trade
   c. AAAI
   d. A4e


3. A _____, in business matters, is an entity that is controlled by a bigger and more powerful entity. The controlled entity is called a company, corporation, or limited liability company and in some cases can be a government or state-owned enterprise, and the controlling entity is called its parent (or the parent company.) The reason for this distinction is that a lone company cannot be a _____ of any organization; only an entity representing a legal fiction as a separate entity can be a _____.
   a. 33 Strategies of War
   b. Subsidiary
   c. 1990 Clean Air Act
   d. 28-hour day


4. _____ is exchanging goods or services that are paid for, in whole or part, with other goods or services.

## Chapter 7. Modes of Entry into Foreign Markets

There are five main variants of _____:

- Barter: Exchange of goods or services directly for other goods or services without the use of money as means of purchase or payment.
- Switch trading: Practice in which one company sells to another its obligation to make a purchase in a given country.
- Counter purchase: Sale of goods and services to a country by a company that promises to make a future purchase of a specific product from the country.
- Buyback: occurs when a firm builds a plant in a country - or supplies technology, equipment, training, or other services to the country and agrees to take a certain percentage of the plant's output as partial payment for the contract.
- Offset: Agreement that a company will offset a hard - currency purchase of an unspecified product from that nation in the future. Agreement by one nation to buy a product from another, subject to the purchase of some or all of the components and raw materials from the buyer of the finished product, or the assembly of such product in the buyer nation.

_____ also occurs when countries lack sufficient hard currency, or when other types of market trade are impossible85 a barrel while Iraq oil sales into Asia were valued at about $22 a barrel. In 2001, India agreed to swap 1.5 million tonnes of Iraqi crude under the oil-for-food program.

a. Countertrade
b. Buy-sell agreement
c. Trade credit
d. 1990 Clean Air Act


5. _____ or contract administration is the management of contracts made with customers, vendors, partners, or employees. _____ includes negotiating the terms and conditions in contracts and ensuring compliance with the terms and conditions, as well as documenting and agreeing any changes that may arise during its implementation or execution. It can be summarized as the process of systematically and efficiently managing contract creating, execution, and analysis for the purpose of maximizing financial and operational performance and minimizing risk.
   a. Contract management
   b. 1990 Clean Air Act
   c. World Trade Organization
   d. Network planning and design


6. _____ refers to the methods of practicing and using another person's business philosophy. The franchisor grants the independent operator the right to distribute its products, techniques, and trademarks for a percentage of gross monthly sales and a royalty fee. Various tangibles and intangibles such as national or international advertising, training, and other support services are commonly made available by the franchisor.

a. 28-hour day
b. Franchising
c. ServiceMaster
d. 1990 Clean Air Act

7. Franchising refers to the methods of practicing and using another person's business philosophy. The _____ grants the independent operator the right to distribute its products, techniques, and trademarks for a percentage of gross monthly sales and a royalty fee. Various tangibles and intangibles such as national or international advertising, training, and other support services are commonly made available by the _____.
a. Franchisor
b. 28-hour day
c. ServiceMaster
d. 1990 Clean Air Act

8. _____ is an advertisement in which a particular product specifically mentions a competitor by name for the express purpose of showing why the competitor is inferior to the product naming it.

This should not be confused with parody advertisements, where a fictional product is being advertised for the purpose of poking fun at the particular advertisement, nor should it be confused with the use of a coined brand name for the purpose of comparing the product without actually naming an actual competitor. ('Wikipedia tastes better and is less filling than the Encyclopedia Galactica.')

In the 1980s, during what has been referred to as the cola wars, soft-drink manufacturer Pepsi ran a series of advertisements where people, caught on hidden camera, in a blind taste test, chose Pepsi over rival Coca-Cola.

a. 28-hour day
b. 1990 Clean Air Act
c. 33 Strategies of War
d. Comparative advertising

9. _____ in its classic form is defined as a company from one country making a physical investment into building a factory in another country. It is the establishment of an enterprise by a foreigner. Its definition can be extended to include investments made to acquire lasting interest in enterprises operating outside of the economy of the investor.
a. Business Roundtable
b. Headquarters
c. Compensation methods
d. Foreign direct investment

## Chapter 7. Modes of Entry into Foreign Markets

10. _____ refers to the movement of cash into or out of a business or financial product. It is usually measured during a specified, finite period of time. Measurement of _____ can be used

- to determine a project's rate of return or value. The time of _____s into and out of projects are used as inputs in financial models such as internal rate of return, and net present value.
- to determine problems with a business's liquidity. Being profitable does not necessarily mean being liquid. A company can fail because of a shortage of cash, even while profitable.
- as an alternate measure of a business's profits when it is believed that accrual accounting concepts do not represent economic realities. For example, a company may be notionally profitable but generating little operational cash (as may be the case for a company that barters its products rather than selling for cash.) In such a case, the company may be deriving additional operating cash by issuing shares evaluating default risk, re-investment requirements, etc.

_____ is a generic term used differently depending on the context. It may be defined by users for their own purposes.

a. Gross profit
b. Sweat equity
c. Gross profit margin
d. Cash flow


11. An _____ is a person who has possession of an enterprise and assumes significant accountability for the inherent risks and the outcome. It is an ambitious leader who combines land, labor, and capital to create and market new goods or services. The term is a loanword from French and was first defined by the Irish economist Richard Cantillon.

a. Entrepreneur
b. AAAI
c. A4e
d. A Stake in the Outcome


12. A _____ is an entity formed between two or more parties to undertake economic activity together. The parties agree to create a new entity by both contributing equity, and they then share in the revenues, expenses, and control of the enterprise. The venture can be for one specific project only, or a continuing business relationship such as the Fuji Xerox _____.

a. Patent
b. Civil Rights Act of 1991
c. Meritor Savings Bank v. Vinson
d. Joint venture


13. In decision theory and estimation theory, the _____ of an estimator, $\hat{\theta}$, of an unknown parameter of the distribution, θ, is the expected value of the loss function

$$R(\theta, \hat{\theta}) = \mathbb{E}_\theta L(\theta, \hat{\theta}) = \int L(\theta, \hat{\theta})\, dP_\theta.$$

where $dP_\theta$ is a probability measure parametrized by θ.

- For a scalar parameter θ and a quadratic loss function,

$$L(\theta, \hat{\theta}) = (\theta - \hat{\theta})^2$$

the _____ function becomes the mean squared error of the estimate,

$$R(\theta, \hat{\theta}) = E_\theta (\theta - \hat{\theta})^2$$

- In density estimation, the unknown parameter is probability density itself. The loss function is typically chosen to be a norm in an appropriate function space. For example, for $L^2$ norm,

$$L(f, \hat{f}) = \|f - \hat{f}\|_2^2$$

the _____ function becomes the mean integrated squared error

$$R(f, \hat{f}) = E\|f - \hat{f}\|^2$$

a. Financial modeling
b. Linear model
c. Risk aversion
d. Risk


14. _____ is one of the managerial functions like planning, organizing, staffing and directing. It is an important function because it helps to check the errors and to take the corrective action so that deviation from standards are minimized and stated goals of the organization are achieved in desired manner. According to modern concepts, _____ is a foreseeing action whereas earlier concept of _____ was used only when errors were detected. _____ in management means setting standards, measuring actual performance and taking corrective action.
   a. Schedule of reinforcement
   b. Decision tree pruning
   c. Turnover
   d. Control

15. _____ consists of the mental process of thinking involved with the process of judging the merits of multiple options and selecting one of them for action. Some simple examples include deciding whether to get up in the morning or go back to sleep, or selecting a given route for a journey. More complex examples (often decisions that affect what a person thinks or their core beliefs) include choosing a lifestyle, religious affiliation, or political position.

   a. Groups decision making
   b. Trade study
   c. Choice
   d. Championship mobilization

16. _____ is the state or fact of exclusive rights and control over property, which may be an object, land/real estate or intellectual property. An _____ right is also referred to as title. The concept of _____ has existed for thousands of years and in all cultures.

   a. Emanation of the state
   b. A Stake in the Outcome
   c. A4e
   d. Ownership

17. A _____ or transnational corporation is a corporation or enterprise that manages production or delivers services in more than one country. It can also be referred to as an international corporation.

   The first modern _____ is generally thought to be the Dutch East India Company, established in 1602.

   a. Command center
   b. Multinational corporation
   c. Financial Accounting Standards Board
   d. Small and medium enterprises

18. _____ in its literal sense is the process of transformation of local or regional phenomena into global ones. It can be described as a process by which the people of the world are unified into a single society and function together.

   This process is a combination of economic, technological, sociocultural and political forces.

   a. Collaborative Planning, Forecasting and Replenishment
   b. Histogram
   c. Cost Management
   d. Globalization

## Chapter 8. Managing International Collaborative Initiatives

1. A _____ is a formal relationship between two or more parties to pursue a set of agreed upon goals or to meet a critical business need while remaining independent organizations.

Partners may provide the _____ with resources such as products, distribution channels, manufacturing capability, project funding, capital equipment, knowledge, expertise, or intellectual property. The alliance is a cooperation or collaboration which aims for a synergy where each partner hopes that the benefits from the alliance will be greater than those from individual efforts.

   a. Farmshoring
   b. Golden parachute
   c. Strategic alliance
   d. Process automation

2. A _____ is one of several ways of doing research whether it is social science related or even socially related. It is an intensive study of a single group, incident, or community.Other ways include experiments, surveys, multiple histories, and analysis of archival information .

Rather than using samples and following a rigid protocol to examine limited number of variables, _____ methods involve an in-depth, longitudinal examination of a single instance or event: a case.

   a. Case study
   b. 1990 Clean Air Act
   c. Standard operating procedure
   d. Longitudinal study

3. A _____ is an entity formed between two or more parties to undertake economic activity together. The parties agree to create a new entity by both contributing equity, and they then share in the revenues, expenses, and control of the enterprise. The venture can be for one specific project only, or a continuing business relationship such as the Fuji Xerox _____.
   a. Meritor Savings Bank v. Vinson
   b. Patent
   c. Civil Rights Act of 1991
   d. Joint venture

4. An _____ is a person who has possession of an enterprise and assumes significant accountability for the inherent risks and the outcome. It is an ambitious leader who combines land, labor, and capital to create and market new goods or services. The term is a loanword from French and was first defined by the Irish economist Richard Cantillon.

a. A4e
b. A Stake in the Outcome
c. AAAI
d. Entrepreneur

5. The phrase mergers and _____s refers to the aspect of corporate strategy, corporate finance and management dealing with the buying, selling and combining of different companies that can aid, finance, or help a growing company in a given industry grow rapidly without having to create another business entity.

An _____, also known as a takeover or a buyout, is the buying of one company (the 'target') by another. An _____ may be friendly or hostile.

a. A4e
b. A Stake in the Outcome
c. AAAI
d. Acquisition

6. _____ is one of the managerial functions like planning, organizing, staffing and directing. It is an important function because it helps to check the errors and to take the corrective action so that deviation from standards are minimized and stated goals of the organization are achieved in desired manner. According to modern concepts, _____ is a foreseeing action whereas earlier concept of _____ was used only when errors were detected. _____ in management means setting standards, measuring actual performance and taking corrective action.

a. Turnover
b. Decision tree pruning
c. Control
d. Schedule of reinforcement

7. _____ is a range of processes aimed at alleviating or eliminating sources of conflict. The term '_____' is sometimes used interchangeably with the term dispute resolution or alternative dispute resolution. Processes of _____ generally include negotiation, mediation and diplomacy.

a. 28-hour day
b. Conflict resolution
c. 1990 Clean Air Act
d. 33 Strategies of War

8. In decision theory and estimation theory, the _____ of an estimator, $\hat{\theta}$, of an unknown parameter of the distribution, θ, is the expected value of the loss function

$$R(\theta, \hat{\theta}) = \mathbb{E}_\theta L(\theta, \hat{\theta}) = \int L(\theta, \hat{\theta})\, dP_\theta.$$

where $dP_\theta$ is a probability measure parametrized by $\theta$.

- For a scalar parameter $\theta$ and a quadratic loss function,

$$L(\theta, \hat{\theta}) = (\theta - \hat{\theta})^2$$

the _____ function becomes the mean squared error of the estimate,

$$R(\theta, \hat{\theta}) = E_\theta (\theta - \hat{\theta})^2$$

- In density estimation, the unknown parameter is probability density itself. The loss function is typically chosen to be a norm in an appropriate function space. For example, for $L^2$ norm,

$$L(f, \hat{f}) = \|f - \hat{f}\|_2^2$$

the _____ function becomes the mean integrated squared error

$$R(f, \hat{f}) = E\|f - \hat{f}\|^2$$

a. Risk
b. Financial modeling
c. Linear model
d. Risk aversion


9. _____ is the state or fact of exclusive rights and control over property, which may be an object, land/real estate or intellectual property. An _____ right is also referred to as title. The concept of _____ has existed for thousands of years and in all cultures.
a. A4e
b. A Stake in the Outcome
c. Emanation of the state
d. Ownership

## Chapter 9. Organizing International Operations

1. A _____ is one of several ways of doing research whether it is social science related or even socially related. It is an intensive study of a single group, incident, or community. Other ways include experiments, surveys, multiple histories, and analysis of archival information.

Rather than using samples and following a rigid protocol to examine limited number of variables, _____ methods involve an in-depth, longitudinal examination of a single instance or event: a case.

 a. Longitudinal study
 b. Standard operating procedure
 c. 1990 Clean Air Act
 d. Case study


2. The 'business case for _____', theorizes that in a global marketplace, a company that employs a diverse workforce (both men and women, people of many generations, people from ethnically and racially diverse backgrounds etc.) is better able to understand the demographics of the marketplace it serves and is thus better equipped to thrive in that marketplace than a company that has a more limited range of employee demographics.

An additional corollary suggests that a company that supports the _____ of its workforce can also improve employee satisfaction, productivity and retention.

 a. Virtual team
 b. Trademark
 c. Diversity
 d. Kanban


3. An _____, or organogram(me)) is a diagram that shows the structure of an organization and the relationships and relative ranks of its parts and positions/jobs. The term is also used for similar diagrams, for example ones showing the different elements of a field of knowledge or a group of languages. The French Encyclopédie had one of the first _____s of knowledge in general.
 a. Organizational chart
 b. A Stake in the Outcome
 c. AAAI
 d. A4e

## Chapter 10. Controlling International Strategies and Operations

1. A _____ is one of several ways of doing research whether it is social science related or even socially related. It is an intensive study of a single group, incident, or community. Other ways include experiments, surveys, multiple histories, and analysis of archival information.

Rather than using samples and following a rigid protocol to examine limited number of variables, _____ methods involve an in-depth, longitudinal examination of a single instance or event: a case.

   a. Longitudinal study
   b. 1990 Clean Air Act
   c. Standard operating procedure
   d. Case study


2. _____ is one of the managerial functions like planning, organizing, staffing and directing. It is an important function because it helps to check the errors and to take the corrective action so that deviation from standards are minimized and stated goals of the organization are achieved in desired manner. According to modern concepts, _____ is a foreseeing action whereas earlier concept of _____ was used only when errors were detected. _____ in management means setting standards, measuring actual performance and taking corrective action.
   a. Schedule of reinforcement
   b. Decision tree pruning
   c. Turnover
   d. Control


3. _____ generally refers to a list of all planned expenses and revenues. It is a plan for saving and spending. A _____ is an important concept in microeconomics, which uses a _____ line to illustrate the trade-offs between two or more goods.
   a. 28-hour day
   b. 1990 Clean Air Act
   c. 33 Strategies of War
   d. Budget


4. In decision theory and estimation theory, the _____ of an estimator, $\hat{\theta}$, of an unknown parameter of the distribution, θ, is the expected value of the loss function

$$R(\theta, \hat{\theta}) = \mathbb{E}_\theta L(\theta, \hat{\theta}) = \int L(\theta, \hat{\theta}) \, dP_\theta.$$

## Chapter 10. Controlling International Strategies and Operations

where $dP_\theta$ is a probability measure parametrized by θ.

- For a scalar parameter θ and a quadratic loss function,

$$L(\theta, \hat{\theta}) = (\theta - \hat{\theta})^2$$

the _____ function becomes the mean squared error of the estimate,

$$R(\theta, \hat{\theta}) = E_\theta(\theta - \hat{\theta})^2$$

- In density estimation, the unknown parameter is probability density itself. The loss function is typically chosen to be a norm in an appropriate function space. For example, for $L^2$ norm,

$$L(f, \hat{f}) = \|f - \hat{f}\|_2^2$$

the _____ function becomes the mean integrated squared error

$$R(f, \hat{f}) = E\|f - \hat{f}\|^2$$

a. Risk aversion
b. Financial modeling
c. Linear model
d. Risk

5. A _____, in business matters, is an entity that is controlled by a bigger and more powerful entity. The controlled entity is called a company, corporation, or limited liability company and in some cases can be a government or state-owned enterprise, and the controlling entity is called its parent (or the parent company.) The reason for this distinction is that a lone company cannot be a _____ of any organization; only an entity representing a legal fiction as a separate entity can be a _____.

a. 33 Strategies of War
b. 28-hour day
c. Subsidiary
d. 1990 Clean Air Act

6. A _____ is a formal relationship between two or more parties to pursue a set of agreed upon goals or to meet a critical business need while remaining independent organizations.

Partners may provide the _____ with resources such as products, distribution channels, manufacturing capability, project funding, capital equipment, knowledge, expertise, or intellectual property. The alliance is a cooperation or collaboration which aims for a synergy where each partner hopes that the benefits from the alliance will be greater than those from individual efforts.

a. Golden parachute
b. Process automation
c. Strategic alliance
d. Farmshoring


7. _____ is a dynamic of being mutually and physically responsible to and sharing a common set of principles with others. This concept differs distinctly from 'dependence' in that an interdependent relationship implies that all participants are emotionally, economically, ecologically and or morally 'interdependent.' Some people advocate freedom or independence as a sort of ultimate good; others do the same with devotion to one's family, community, or society. _____ recognizes the truth in each position and weaves them together.

a. A4e
b. A Stake in the Outcome
c. AAAI
d. Interdependence

## Chapter 11. Managing Technology and Knowledge

1. A _____ is one of several ways of doing research whether it is social science related or even socially related. It is an intensive study of a single group, incident, or community. Other ways include experiments, surveys, multiple histories, and analysis of archival information.

Rather than using samples and following a rigid protocol to examine limited number of variables, _____ methods involve an in-depth, longitudinal examination of a single instance or event: a case.

   a. Longitudinal study
   b. Standard operating procedure
   c. 1990 Clean Air Act
   d. Case study

2. _____ is the process of sharing of skills, knowledge, technologies, methods of manufacturing, samples of manufacturing and facilities among governments and other institutions to ensure that scientific and technological developments are accessible to a wider range of users who can then further develop and exploit the technology into new products, processes, applications, materials or services. It is closely related to (and may arguably be considered a subset of) Knowledge transfer. Related terms, used almost synonymously, include 'technology valorisation' and 'technology commercialisation'.

   a. Technology transfer
   b. Munn v. Illinois
   c. Mediation
   d. Competition law

3. Organizational culture is not the same as _____. It is wider and deeper concepts, something that an organization 'is' rather than what it 'has' (according to Buchanan and Huczynski.)

   _____ is the total sum of the values, customs, traditions and meanings that make a company unique.

   a. Corporate culture
   b. Path-goal theory
   c. Work design
   d. Job analysis

4. Recent strategic thought points ever more clearly towards the conclusion that the critical strategic question is not 'What?,' but 'Why?' The work of Mintzberg and others who draw a distinction between strategic planning (defined as systematic programming of pre-identified strategies) and _____ supports that conclusion. Intensified exploration of strategy from new directions is now coming together in the concept of what is being called _____. At this point, there is no generally accepted definition of the term, no common agreement as to its role or importance, and no standardized list of key competencies of strategic thinkers.

## Chapter 11. Managing Technology and Knowledge

a. Strategic thinking
b. Switching cost
c. Complementors
d. Strategic drift

5. A _____ is a process in which a potential employee is evaluated by an employer for prospective employment in their company, organization and was established in the late 16th century.

A _____ typically precedes the hiring decision, and is used to evaluate the candidate. The interview is usually preceded by the evaluation of submitted résumés from interested candidates, then selecting a small number of candidates for interviews.

a. Payrolling
b. Split shift
c. Job interview
d. Supported employment

6. The _____ is a concept from business management that was first described and popularized by Michael Porter in his 1985 best-seller, Competitive Advantage: Creating and Sustaining Superior Performance.

A _____ is a chain of activities. Products pass through all activities of the chain in order and at each activity the product gains some value. The chain of activities gives the products more added value than the sum of added values of all activities. It is important not to mix the concept of the _____ with the costs occurring throughout the activities.

a. Customer relationship management
b. Value chain
c. Mass marketing
d. Market development

7. The term _____ collectively refers to all resources that determine the value and the competitiveness of an enterprise. As such, it includes as subsets the attributes that concur to building all financial statements as well as the balance sheet.
a. A Stake in the Outcome
b. Intellectual capital
c. AAAI
d. A4e

## Chapter 11. Managing Technology and Knowledge

8. _____ is the process by which a new idea or new product is accepted by the market. The rate of _____ is the speed that the new idea spreads from one consumer to the next. Adoption is similar to _____ except that it deals with the psychological processes an individual goes through, rather than an aggregate market process.

   a. Value chain
   b. Category management
   c. Mass marketing
   d. Diffusion

9. A _____ is the term given to a company that facilitates the learning of its members and continuously transforms itself. _____s develop as a result of the pressures facing modern organizations and enables them to remain competitive in the business environment. A _____ has five main features; systems thinking, personal mastery, mental models, shared vision and team learning.

   a. Quality function deployment
   b. Learning organization
   c. 1990 Clean Air Act
   d. Hoshin Kanri

10. A _____ is a name or trademark connected with a product or producer. _____s have become increasingly important components of culture and the economy, now being described as 'cultural accessories and personal philosophies'.

    Some people distinguish the psychological aspect of a _____ from the experiential aspect.

    a. Brand
    b. Brand loyalty
    c. Brand awareness
    d. Brand extension

11. _____ refers to the overarching strategy of the diversified firm. Such a _____ answers the questions of 'in which businesses should we be in?' and 'how does being in these business create synergy and/or add to the competitive advantage of the corporation as a whole?'

Business strategy refers to the aggregated strategies of single business firm or a strategic business unit (SBU) in a diversified corporation. According to Michael Porter, a firm must formulate a business strategy that incorporates either cost leadership, differentiation or focus in order to achieve a sustainable competitive advantage and long-term success in its chosen arenas or industries.

a. Strategic group
b. Competitive heterogeneity
c. Strategic drift
d. Corporate strategy

## Chapter 12. Communicating across Borders and Cultures

1. A _____ is one of several ways of doing research whether it is social science related or even socially related. It is an intensive study of a single group, incident, or community. Other ways include experiments, surveys, multiple histories, and analysis of archival information.

Rather than using samples and following a rigid protocol to examine limited number of variables, _____ methods involve an in-depth, longitudinal examination of a single instance or event: a case.

   a. Longitudinal study
   b. 1990 Clean Air Act
   c. Standard operating procedure
   d. Case study

2. The term _____ was introduced by anthropologist Edward T. Hall in 1966 to describe set measurable distances between people as they interact. The effects of _____, according to Hall, can be summarized by the following loose rule:

According to Jonathon Tabor distance-spacing theories based on the early animal-like human of German zoologist Heini Hediger, as found in his 1955 book Studies of the Behavior of Captive Animals in Zoos and Circuses. Hediger, in animals, had distinguished between flight distance, critical distance (attack boundary), personal distance (distance separating members of non-contact species, as a pair of swans), and social distance (intraspecies communication distance.)

   a. 1990 Clean Air Act
   b. 33 Strategies of War
   c. 28-hour day
   d. Proxemics

3. _____ is both the conscious and unconscious act of revealing more about ourselves to others. This may include but is not limited to thoughts, feelings, aspirations, goals, failures, successes, fears, dreams as well as our likes, dislikes, and favorites. Many people attempt to avoid 'self-disclosing' too much to coworkers, or when dating for fear of being judged negatively by others.
   a. Soft skill
   b. Social network analysis
   c. Social influence
   d. Self-disclosure

## Chapter 13. Negotiation and Decision Making across Borders and Cultures

1. A _____ is one of several ways of doing research whether it is social science related or even socially related. It is an intensive study of a single group, incident, or community. Other ways include experiments, surveys, multiple histories, and analysis of archival information.

Rather than using samples and following a rigid protocol to examine limited number of variables, _____ methods involve an in-depth, longitudinal examination of a single instance or event: a case.

   a. Longitudinal study
   b. Standard operating procedure
   c. 1990 Clean Air Act
   d. Case study


2. _____ is a form of social influence. It is the process of guiding people and oneself toward the adoption of an idea, attitude, or action by rational and symbolic (though not always logical) means. It is strategy of problem-solving relying on 'appeals' rather than coercion.
   a. Self-enhancement
   b. Social loafing
   c. Personal space
   d. Persuasion


3. The _____ of 1977 (15 U.S.C. §§ 78dd-1, et seq.) is a United States federal law known primarily for two of its main provisions, one that addresses accounting transparency requirements under the Securities Exchange Act of 1934 and another concerning bribery of foreign officials.
   a. Meritor Savings Bank v. Vinson
   b. Foreign Corrupt Practices Act
   c. Social Security Act of 1965
   d. Limited liability


4. _____ can be regarded as an outcome of mental processes (cognitive process) leading to the selection of a course of action among several alternatives. Every _____ process produces a final choice. The output can be an action or an opinion of choice.
   a. 28-hour day
   b. 33 Strategies of War
   c. 1990 Clean Air Act
   d. Decision making


5. _____ is a range of processes aimed at alleviating or eliminating sources of conflict. The term '_____' is sometimes used interchangeably with the term dispute resolution or alternative dispute resolution. Processes of _____ generally include negotiation, mediation and diplomacy.

a. 33 Strategies of War
b. 1990 Clean Air Act
c. 28-hour day
d. Conflict resolution

## Chapter 14. Work Motivation across Cultures and Borders

1. A _____ is one of several ways of doing research whether it is social science related or even socially related. It is an intensive study of a single group, incident, or community. Other ways include experiments, surveys, multiple histories, and analysis of archival information.

Rather than using samples and following a rigid protocol to examine limited number of variables, _____ methods involve an in-depth, longitudinal examination of a single instance or event: a case.

   a. Standard operating procedure
   b. Case study
   c. 1990 Clean Air Act
   d. Longitudinal study


2. Clayton Paul Alderfer is an American psychologist who further expanded Maslow's hierarchy of needs by categorizing the hierarchy into his _____ Alderfer categorized the lower order needs (Physiological and Safety) into the Existence category. He fit Maslow's interpersonal love and esteem needs into the relatedness category. The growth category contained the Self Actualization and self esteem needs.

Alderfer also proposed a regression theory to go along with the _____. He said that when needs in a higher category are not met then individuals redouble the efforts invested in a lower category need.

   a. Adam Smith
   b. Alvin Neill Jackson
   c. ERG theory
   d. Abraham Harold Maslow


3. _____ was developed by Frederick Herzberg, a psychologist who found that job satisfaction and job dissatisfaction acted independently of each other. _____ states that there are certain factors in the workplace that cause job satisfaction, while a separate set of factors cause dissatisfaction.
   a. Need for power
   b. Need for Achievement
   c. 1990 Clean Air Act
   d. Two-factor theory


4. _____ refers to an individual's desire for significant accomplishment, mastering of skills, control, or high standards. The term was introduced by the psychologist, David McClelland.

   _____ is related to the difficulty of tasks people choose to undertake.

a. 1990 Clean Air Act
b. Two-factor theory
c. Need for power
d. Need for achievement

5. The _____ is a term that was popularised by David McClelland and describes a person's need to feel a sense of involvement and 'belonging' within a social group. However, it should be recognised that McClellend's thinking was strongly influenced by the pioneering work of Henry Murray who first identified underlying psychological human needs and motivational processes (1938.) It was Murray who set out a taxonomy of needs, including Achievement, Power and Affiliation - and placed these in the context of an integrated motivational model.
   a. Polynomial conjoint measurement
   b. Strong-Campbell Interest Inventory
   c. Need for affiliation
   d. SESAMO

6. _____ is a term that was popularized by renowned psychologist David McClelland in 1961. However, it should be recognized that McClellend's thinking was strongly influenced by the pioneering work of Henry Murray who first identified underlying psychological human needs and motivational processes (1938.) It was Murray who set out a taxonomy of needs, including Achievement, Power and Affiliation - and placed these in the context of an integrated motivational model.
   a. Two-factor theory
   b. 1990 Clean Air Act
   c. Need for power
   d. Need for Achievement

7. In law, _____ is the term to describe a partnership between two or more parties.

In England a number of statutes on the subject have been passed, the chief being the Bastardy Act of 1845, and the Bastardy Laws Amendment Acts of 1872 and 1873. The mother of a bastard may summon the putative father to petty sessions within twelve months of the birth (or at any later time if he is proved to have contributed to the child's support within twelve months after the birth), and the justices, as after hearing evidence on both sides, may, if the mother's evidence be corroborated in some material particular, adjudge the man to be the putative father of the child, and order him to pay a sum not exceeding five shillings a week for its maintenance, together with a sum for expenses incidental to the birth, or the funeral expenses, if it has died before the date of order, and the costs of the proceedings.

a. Affiliation
b. Abraham Harold Maslow
c. Adam Smith
d. Affiliation

8. _____ is about the mental processes regarding choice, or choosing. It explains the processes that an individual undergoes to make choices. In organizational behavior study, _____ is a motivation theory first proposed by Victor Vroom of the Yale School of Management.
   a. Expectancy theory
   b. A Stake in the Outcome
   c. AAAI
   d. A4e

9. _____ attempts to explain relational satisfaction in terms of perceptions of fair/unfair distributions of resources within interpersonal relationships. _____ is considered as one of the justice theories, It was first developed in 1962 by John Stacey Adams, a workplace and behavioral psychologist, who asserted that employees seek to maintain equity between the inputs that they bring to a job and the outcomes that they receive from it against the perceived inputs and outcomes of others (Adams, 1965.) The belief is that people value fair treatment which causes them to be motivated to keep the fairness maintained within the relationships of their co-workers and the organization.
   a. AAAI
   b. A Stake in the Outcome
   c. Equity theory
   d. A4e

10. _____ has become one of the most popular theories in organizational psychology.

Goal setting has been a formula used for acheivement since the early 1800s. The form and pattern has cahanged drastically over the years and there is still much debate as to what is the most efective pattern to follow.

   a. Corporate Culture
   b. Human relations
   c. Job satisfaction
   d. Goal-setting theory

11. Within graph theory and network analysis, there are various measures of the _____ of a vertex within a graph that determine the relative importance of a vertex within the graph (for example, how important a person is within a social network, or, in the theory of space syntax, how important a room is within a building or how well-used a road is within an urban network.)

There are four measures of _____ that are widely used in network analysis: degree _____, betweenness, closeness, and eigenvector _____.

The first, and simplest, is degree _____.

a. 1990 Clean Air Act
b. 33 Strategies of War
c. 28-hour day
d. Centrality


12. _____ is a term in psychology which refers to a person's belief about what causes the good or bad results in his or her life, either in general or in a specific area such as health or academics. Understanding of the concept was developed by Julian B. Rotter in 1954, and has since become an important aspect of personality studies.

_____ refers to the extent to which individuals believe that they can control events that affect them.

a. Machiavellianism
b. Social loafing
c. Self-enhancement
d. Locus of control


13. _____ is one of the managerial functions like planning, organizing, staffing and directing. It is an important function because it helps to check the errors and to take the corrective action so that deviation from standards are minimized and stated goals of the organization are achieved in desired manner. According to modern concepts, _____ is a foreseeing action whereas earlier concept of _____ was used only when errors were detected. _____ in management means setting standards, measuring actual performance and taking corrective action.

a. Turnover
b. Decision tree pruning
c. Schedule of reinforcement
d. Control


14. _____ is a term used to describe any moral, political that stresses human interdependence and the importance of a collective, rather than the importance of separate individuals. Collectivists focus on community and society, and seek to give priority to group goals over individual goals. The philosophical underpinnings of _____ are for some related to holism or organicism - the view that the whole is greater than the sum of its parts/pieces.

a. 28-hour day
b. Collaborative methods
c. 1990 Clean Air Act
d. Collectivism

15. _____ describes how content an individual is with his or her job.

The happier people are within their job, the more satisfied they are said to be. _____ is not the same as motivation, although it is clearly linked.

a. Human relations
b. Job analysis
c. Goal-setting theory
d. Job satisfaction

## Chapter 15. Leadership across Borders and Cultures

1. _____ has been described as the 'process of social influence in which one person can enlist the aid and support of others in the accomplishment of a common task'. A definition more inclusive of followers comes from Alan Keith of Genentech who said '_____ is ultimately about creating a way for people to contribute to making something extraordinary happen.'

   _____ is one of the most salient aspects of the organizational context. However, defining _____ has been challenging.

   a. 28-hour day
   b. 1990 Clean Air Act
   c. Situational leadership
   d. Leadership


2. A _____ is one of several ways of doing research whether it is social science related or even socially related. It is an intensive study of a single group, incident, or community. Other ways include experiments, surveys, multiple histories, and analysis of archival information.

   Rather than using samples and following a rigid protocol to examine limited number of variables, _____ methods involve an in-depth, longitudinal examination of a single instance or event: a case.

   a. Standard operating procedure
   b. Longitudinal study
   c. 1990 Clean Air Act
   d. Case study


3. _____ refers to the movement of cash into or out of a business or financial product. It is usually measured during a specified, finite period of time. Measurement of _____ can be used

   - to determine a project's rate of return or value. The time of _____s into and out of projects are used as inputs in financial models such as internal rate of return, and net present value.
   - to determine problems with a business's liquidity. Being profitable does not necessarily mean being liquid. A company can fail because of a shortage of cash, even while profitable.
   - as an alternate measure of a business's profits when it is believed that accrual accounting concepts do not represent economic realities. For example, a company may be notionally profitable but generating little operational cash (as may be the case for a company that barters its products rather than selling for cash.) In such a case, the company may be deriving additional operating cash by issuing shares evaluating default risk, re-investment requirements, etc.

   _____ is a generic term used differently depending on the context. It may be defined by users for their own purposes.

## Chapter 15. Leadership across Borders and Cultures

a. Gross profit margin
b. Gross profit
c. Sweat equity
d. Cash flow

4. The _____ is a leadership theory in the field of organizational studies developed by Robert House in 1971 and revised in 1996. The theory that a leader's behavior is contingent to the satisfaction, motivation and performance of subordinates. The revised version also argues that the leader engage in behaviors that complement subordinate's abilities and compensate for deficiencies.
   a. Path-goal theory
   b. Human relations
   c. Corporate Culture
   d. Sociotechnical systems

5. _____ is a leadership style that defines as leadership that creates voluble and positive change in the followers. A transformational leader focuses on 'transforming' others to help each other, to look out for each other, be encouraging, harmonious, and look out for the organization as a whole. In this leadership, the leader enhances the motivation, moral and performance of his follower group.
   a. SESAMO
   b. Polynomial conjoint measurement
   c. Strong-Campbell Interest Inventory
   d. Transformational leadership

6. A _____ is a list of the general tasks and responsibilities of a position. Typically, it also includes to whom the position reports, specifications such as the qualifications needed by the person in the job, salary range for the position, etc. A _____ is usually developed by conducting a job analysis, which includes examining the tasks and sequences of tasks necessary to perform the job.
   a. Recruitment advertising
   b. Recruitment Process Insourcing
   c. Recruitment
   d. Job description

7. A _____ is a volunteer group composed of workers (or even students), usually under the leadership of their supervisor (but they can elect a team leader), who are trained to identify, analyse and solve work-related problems and present their solutions to management in order to improve the performance of the organization, and motivate and enrich the work of employees. When matured, true _____s become self-managing, having gained the confidence of management. _____s are an alternative to the dehumanising concept of the Division of Labour, where workers or individuals are treated like robots.

a. Quality circle
b. Competency-based job descriptions
c. Certified in Production and Inventory Management
d. Connectionist expert systems


8. _____ is the concept of how effective an organization is in achieving the outcomes the organization intends to produce. The idea of _____ is especially important for non-profit organizations as most people who donate money to non-profit organizations and charities are interested in knowing whether the organization is effective in accomplishing its goals.

An organization's effectiveness is also dependent on its communicative competence and ethics.

a. Organizational structure
b. Informal organization
c. Organizational Effectiveness
d. Organizational development


9. _____ is a range of processes aimed at alleviating or eliminating sources of conflict. The term '_____' is sometimes used interchangeably with the term dispute resolution or alternative dispute resolution. Processes of _____ generally include negotiation, mediation and diplomacy.
a. 1990 Clean Air Act
b. 28-hour day
c. 33 Strategies of War
d. Conflict resolution

## Chapter 16. International Human Resources Management

1. A _____ is one of several ways of doing research whether it is social science related or even socially related. It is an intensive study of a single group, incident, or community. Other ways include experiments, surveys, multiple histories, and analysis of archival information.

Rather than using samples and following a rigid protocol to examine limited number of variables, _____ methods involve an in-depth, longitudinal examination of a single instance or event: a case.

a. 1990 Clean Air Act
b. Longitudinal study
c. Standard operating procedure
d. Case study

2. In decision theory and estimation theory, the _____ of an estimator, $\hat{\theta}$, of an unknown parameter of the distribution, θ, is the expected value of the loss function

$$R(\theta,\hat{\theta}) = \mathbb{E}_\theta L(\theta,\hat{\theta}) = \int L(\theta,\hat{\theta})\, dP_\theta.$$

where $dP_\theta$ is a probability measure parametrized by θ.

- For a scalar parameter θ and a quadratic loss function,

$$L(\theta,\hat{\theta}) = (\theta - \hat{\theta})^2$$

the _____ function becomes the mean squared error of the estimate,

$$R(\theta,\hat{\theta}) = E_\theta(\theta - \hat{\theta})^2$$

- In density estimation, the unknown parameter is probability density itself. The loss function is typically chosen to be a norm in an appropriate function space. For example, for $L^2$ norm,

$$L(f,\hat{f}) = \|f - \hat{f}\|_2^2$$

the _____ function becomes the mean integrated squared error

$$R(f,\hat{f}) = E\|f - \hat{f}\|^2$$

a. Risk aversion
b. Risk
c. Financial modeling
d. Linear model


3. _____ is one of the managerial functions like planning, organizing, staffing and directing. It is an important function because it helps to check the errors and to take the corrective action so that deviation from standards are minimized and stated goals of the organization are achieved in desired manner. According to modern concepts, _____ is a foreseeing action whereas earlier concept of _____ was used only when errors were detected. _____ in management means setting standards, measuring actual performance and taking corrective action.
   a. Turnover
   b. Schedule of reinforcement
   c. Decision tree pruning
   d. Control


4. _____ refers to the process of screening, and selecting qualified people for a job at an organization or firm mid- and large-size organizations and companies often retain professional recruiters or outsource some of the process to _____ agencies. External _____ is the process of attracting and selecting employees from outside the organization.

The _____ industry has four main types of agencies: employment agencies, _____ websites and job search engines, 'headhunters' for executive and professional _____, and in-house _____.

   a. Recruitment Process Outsourcing
   b. Recruitment
   c. Labour hire
   d. Referral recruitment


5. An _____ is a person temporarily or permanently residing in a country and culture other than that of the person's upbringing or legal residence. The word comes from the Latin ex and patria (country, fatherland.)

The term is sometimes used in the context of Westerners living in non-Western countries, although it is also used to describe Westerners living in other Western countries, such as Americans living in the United Kingdom, or Britons living in Spain.

## Chapter 16. International Human Resources Management

   a. A4e
   b. Expatriate
   c. AAAI
   d. A Stake in the Outcome

6. A _____ or maquila is a factory that imports materials and equipment on a duty-free and tariff-free basis for assembly or manufacturing and then re-exports the assembled product, usually back to the originating country. A maquila is also referred to as a 'twin plant', or 'in-bond' industry. Nearly half a million Mexicans are employed in _____ s.
   a. 1990 Clean Air Act
   b. 28-hour day
   c. 33 Strategies of War
   d. Maquiladora

7. _____ is an increasingly broadening term with which an organization, or other human system describes the combination of traditionally administrative personnel functions with acquisition and application of skills, knowledge and experience, Employee Relations and resource planning at various levels. The field draws upon concepts developed in Industrial/Organizational Psychology and System Theory. _____ has at least two related interpretations depending on context. The original usage derives from political economy and economics, where it was traditionally called labor, one of four factors of production although this perspective is changing as a function of new and ongoing research into more strategic approaches at national levels. This first usage is used more in terms of '_____ development', and can go beyond just organizations to the level of nations. The more traditional usage within corporations and businesses refers to the individuals within a firm or agency, and to the portion of the organization that deals with hiring, firing, training, and other personnel issues, typically referred to as '_____ management'.
   a. Progressive discipline
   b. Human resource management
   c. Bradford Factor
   d. Human resources

8. In the field of human resource management, _____ is the field concerned with organizational activity aimed at bettering the performance of individuals and groups in organizational settings. It has been known by several names, including employee development, human resource development, and learning and development.

Harrison observes that the name was endlessly debated by the Chartered Institute of Personnel and Development during its review of professional standards in 1999/2000.

a. Performance appraisal
b. Person specification
c. Training and development
d. Revolving door syndrome


9. The field of _____ looks at the relationship between management and workers, particularly groups of workers represented by a union.

_____ is an important factor in analyzing 'varieties of capitalism', such as neocorporatism, social democracy, and neoliberalism

a. Informal organization
b. Industrial relations
c. Organizational effectiveness
d. Overtime


10. In economics, business, retail, and accounting, a _____ is the value of money that has been used up to produce something, and hence is not available for use anymore. In economics, a _____ is an alternative that is given up as a result of a decision. In business, the _____ may be one of acquisition, in which case the amount of money expended to acquire it is counted as _____.
a. Fixed costs
b. Cost allocation
c. Cost overrun
d. Cost


11. _____ denotes the location where most, if not all, of the important functions of an organization are coordinated. The corporate _____ is the entity at the top of a corporation taking full responsibility managing all business activities. In the UK, the term 'head office' is most commonly used for the HQs of large corporations.
a. National Center for Trauma-Informed Care
b. Wells Fargo ' Co.
c. Headquarters
d. Command center


12. In economics and sociology, an _____ is any factor (financial or non-financial) that enables or motivates a particular course of action, or counts as a reason for preferring one choice to the alternatives. It is an expectation that encourages people to behave in a certain way. Since human beings are purposeful creatures, the study of _____ structures is central to the study of all economic activity (both in terms of individual decision-making and in terms of co-operation and competition within a larger institutional structure.)

a. A Stake in the Outcome
b. AAAI
c. A4e
d. Incentive

13. A _____ is a form of periodic payment from an employer to an employee, which may be specified in an employment contract. It is contrasted with piece wages, where each job, hour or other unit is paid separately, rather than on a periodic basis.

From the point of a view of running a business, _____ can also be viewed as the cost of acquiring human resources for running operations, and is then termed personnel expense or _____ expense.

a. Training and development
b. Salary
c. Human resource management
d. Human resources

14. _____ is, in very basic words, a position a firm occupies against its competitors.

According to Michael Porter, the three methods for creating a sustainable _____ are through:

1. Cost leadership

2. Differentiation

3. Focus (economics)

a. Theory Z
b. 28-hour day
c. 1990 Clean Air Act
d. Competitive advantage

15. In economics, _____ refers to the ability of a person or a country to produce a particular good at a lower marginal cost and opportunity cost than another person or country. It is the ability to produce a product most efficiently given all the other products that could be produced. It can be contrasted with absolute advantage which refers to the ability of a person or a country to produce a particular good at a lower absolute cost than another.

a. 33 Strategies of War
b. 1990 Clean Air Act
c. 28-hour day
d. Comparative advantage

# Chapter 17. Ethics and Social Responsibility for International Firms

1. _____ is a form of corporate self-regulation integrated into a business model. Ideally, _____ policy would function as a built-in, self-regulating mechanism whereby business would monitor and ensure their adherence to law, ethical standards, and international norms. Business would embrace responsibility for the impact of their activities on the environment, consumers, employees, communities, stakeholders and all other members of the public sphere.
   a. Corporate social responsibility
   b. 28-hour day
   c. 1990 Clean Air Act
   d. 33 Strategies of War

2. _____ is an increasingly broadening term with which an organization, or other human system describes the combination of traditionally administrative personnel functions with acquisition and application of skills, knowledge and experience, Employee Relations and resource planning at various levels. The field draws upon concepts developed in Industrial/Organizational Psychology and System Theory. _____ has at least two related interpretations depending on context. The original usage derives from political economy and economics, where it was traditionally called labor, one of four factors of production although this perspective is changing as a function of new and ongoing research into more strategic approaches at national levels. This first usage is used more in terms of '_____ development', and can go beyond just organizations to the level of nations . The more traditional usage within corporations and businesses refers to the individuals within a firm or agency, and to the portion of the organization that deals with hiring, firing, training, and other personnel issues, typically referred to as `_____ management'.
   a. Progressive discipline
   b. Human resources
   c. Bradford Factor
   d. Human resource management

3. _____ is a broad label that refers to any individuals or households that use goods and services generated within the economy. The concept of a _____ is used in different contexts, so that the usage and significance of the term may vary.

   Typically when business people and economists talk of _____s they are talking about person as _____, an aggregated commodity item with little individuality other than that expressed in the buy/not-buy decision.

   a. Consumer
   b. 33 Strategies of War
   c. 1990 Clean Air Act
   d. 28-hour day

4. _____ laws are designed to ensure fair competition and the free flow of truthful information in the marketplace. The laws are designed to prevent businesses that engage in fraud or specified unfair practices from gaining an advantage over competitors and may provide additional protection for the weak and unable to take care of themselves. _____ laws are a form of government regulation which protects the interests of consumers.

a. Consumer protection
b. Certificate of Incorporation
c. Comprehensive Environmental Response, Compensation, and Liability Act
d. Sarbanes-Oxley Act

5. A _____ is a set of rules outlining the responsibilities of or proper practices for an individual or organization. Related concepts include ethical codes and honor codes.

In its 2007 International Good Practice Guidance, Defining and Developing an Effective _____ for Organizations, the International Federation of Accountants provided the following working definition:

'Principles, values, standards, or rules of behavior that guide the decisions, procedures and systems of an organization in a way that (a) contributes to the welfare of its key stakeholders, and (b) respects the rights of all constituents affected by its operations.'

a. 1990 Clean Air Act
b. 28-hour day
c. 33 Strategies of War
d. Code of conduct

6. _____ is a contract between two parties, one being the employer and the other being the employee. An employee may be defined as: 'A person in the service of another under any contract of hire, express or implied, oral or written, where the employer has the power or right to control and direct the employee in the material details of how the work is to be performed.' Black's Law Dictionary page 471 (5th ed. 1979.)

a. Exit interview
b. Employment rate
c. Employment counsellor
d. Employment

7. In decision theory and estimation theory, the _____ of an estimator, $\hat{\theta}$, of an unknown parameter of the distribution, θ, is the expected value of the loss function

$$R(\theta, \hat{\theta}) = \mathbb{E}_\theta L(\theta, \hat{\theta}) = \int L(\theta, \hat{\theta})\, dP_\theta.$$

# Chapter 17. Ethics and Social Responsibility for International Firms

where $dP_\theta$ is a probability measure parametrized by θ.

- For a scalar parameter θ and a quadratic loss function,

$$L(\theta, \hat{\theta}) = (\theta - \hat{\theta})^2$$

the _____ function becomes the mean squared error of the estimate,

$$R(\theta, \hat{\theta}) = E_\theta(\theta - \hat{\theta})^2$$

- In density estimation, the unknown parameter is probability density itself. The loss function is typically chosen to be a norm in an appropriate function space. For example, for $L^2$ norm,

$$L(f, \hat{f}) = \|f - \hat{f}\|_2^2$$

the _____ function becomes the mean integrated squared error

$$R(f, \hat{f}) = E\|f - \hat{f}\|^2$$

a. Linear model
b. Risk aversion
c. Financial modeling
d. Risk


8. A _____ is typically described as a deliberate plan of action to guide decisions and achieve rational outcome(s.) However, the term may also be used to denote what is actually done, even though it is unplanned.

The term may apply to government, private sector organizations and groups, and individuals.

a. 1990 Clean Air Act
b. Policy
c. 33 Strategies of War
d. 28-hour day

## Chapter 17. Ethics and Social Responsibility for International Firms

9. In economics, business, retail, and accounting, a _____ is the value of money that has been used up to produce something, and hence is not available for use anymore. In economics, a _____ is an alternative that is given up as a result of a decision. In business, the _____ may be one of acquisition, in which case the amount of money expended to acquire it is counted as _____.
   a. Fixed costs
   b. Cost overrun
   c. Cost
   d. Cost allocation


10. Levi Strauss, born Löb Strauss (February 26, 1829 - September 26, 1902) was a German-Jewish immigrant to the United States who founded the first company to manufacture blue jeans. His firm, _____, began in 1853 in San Francisco, California.

    Levi Strauss was born in Bavaria, Germany, to Hirsch Strauss and his wife Rebecca (Haas) Strauss.

    a. Adam Smith
    b. Affiliation
    c. Abraham Harold Maslow
    d. Levi Strauss ' Company


11. A _____ is a working environment with conditions that are considered by many people of industrialized nations to be difficult or dangerous, usually where the workers have few opportunities to address their situation. This can include exposure to harmful materials, hazardous situations, extreme temperatures, or abuse from employers. _____ workers often work long hours for little pay, regardless of any laws mandating overtime pay or a minimum wage.
    a. Rate of return
    b. Continuous
    c. Sweatshop
    d. Complement


12. A _____ is one of several ways of doing research whether it is social science related or even socially related. It is an intensive study of a single group, incident, or community. Other ways include experiments, surveys, multiple histories, and analysis of archival information .

    Rather than using samples and following a rigid protocol to examine limited number of variables, _____ methods involve an in-depth, longitudinal examination of a single instance or event: a case.

a. Case study
b. Standard operating procedure
c. 1990 Clean Air Act
d. Longitudinal study

ANSWER KEY

**Chapter 1**
1. c   2. d   3. c   4. d   5. c   6. d   7. d   8. c   9. a   10. a
11. b   12. b   13. d   14. d   15. d   16. d   17. d   18. d   19. c   20. d
21. b   22. d   23. b   24. d   25. b

**Chapter 2**
1. d   2. d   3. d   4. c   5. d   6. d   7. c   8. a   9. d   10. b
11. d   12. a   13. b   14. d   15. b   16. d   17. b   18. d   19. a   20. c
21. d   22. a   23. d

**Chapter 3**
1. d   2. b   3. b   4. d   5. c   6. a   7. d   8. b   9. d   10. a
11. a   12. d   13. b   14. d   15. d   16. d   17. a

**Chapter 4**
1. d   2. d   3. d   4. b   5. a   6. d   7. d   8. d   9. c   10. d
11. b   12. b   13. d   14. b   15. b

**Chapter 5**
1. d   2. a   3. b   4. c   5. a   6. b   7. a   8. a   9. c   10. a
11. b

**Chapter 6**
1. d   2. a   3. d   4. d   5. d   6. c   7. a   8. b   9. d   10. d
11. a   12. d   13. a   14. d   15. b   16. d   17. c   18. d   19. c   20. d
21. d   22. d   23. d

**Chapter 7**
1. d   2. b   3. b   4. a   5. a   6. b   7. a   8. d   9. d   10. d
11. a   12. d   13. d   14. d   15. c   16. d   17. b   18. d

**Chapter 8**
1. c   2. a   3. d   4. d   5. d   6. c   7. b   8. a   9. d

**Chapter 9**
1. d   2. c   3. a

**Chapter 10**
1. d   2. d   3. d   4. d   5. c   6. c   7. d

**Chapter 11**
1. d   2. a   3. a   4. a   5. c   6. b   7. b   8. d   9. b   10. a
11. d

**Chapter 12**
1. d   2. d   3. d

**Chapter 13**
1. d  2. d  3. b  4. d  5. d

**Chapter 14**
1. b  2. c  3. d  4. d  5. c  6. c  7. a  8. a  9. c  10. d
11. d  12. d  13. d  14. d  15. d

**Chapter 15**
1. d  2. d  3. d  4. a  5. d  6. d  7. a  8. c  9. d

**Chapter 16**
1. d  2. b  3. d  4. b  5. b  6. d  7. d  8. c  9. b  10. d
11. c  12. d  13. b  14. d  15. d

**Chapter 17**
1. a  2. b  3. a  4. a  5. d  6. d  7. d  8. b  9. c  10. d
11. c  12. a